COACH your SENSES

DISCOVER THE **INNER SECRETS OF OUTER SUCCESS**

SIRSHREE

COACH YOUR SENSES

Discover the Inner Secrets of Outer Success
By **Sirshree** Tejparkhi

Copyright © Tejgyan Global Foundation
All Rights Reserved 2022

Tejgyan Global Foundation is a charitable organization
with its headquarters in Pune, India.

ISBN : 978-93-90607-05-1

Published by WOW Publishings Pvt. Ltd., India
First Edition published in July 2022

Printed and bound by Trinity Academy, Pune, INDIA

This book is the translation of the Hindi book titled
"5 Indriyon Ke Coach Kaise Bane" by Sirshree Tejparkhi.

Copyrights are reserved with Tejgyan Global Foundation and publishing rights are vested exclusively with WOW Publishings Pvt. Ltd. This book is sold subject to the condition that it shall not by way of trade or otherwise, be lent, resold, hired out, or otherwise circulated without the publisher's prior written consent in any form of binding or cover other than that in which it is published and without a similar condition including this condition being imposed on the subsequent purchaser and without limiting the rights under copyright reserved above, no part of this publication may be reproduced, stored in or introduced into a retrieval system, or transmitted, in any form, or by any means, electronic, mechanical, photocopying, recording or otherwise, without the prior written permission of both the copyright owner and the above-mentioned publisher of this book. Any person who does any unauthorized act in relation to this publication may be liable to criminal prosecution and civil claims for damages.

Although the author and publisher have made every effort to ensure accuracy of content in this book, they hereby disclaim any liability to any party for any loss, damage, or disruption caused by errors or omissions, resulting from negligence, accident, or any other cause. Readers are advised to take full responsibility to exercise discretion in understanding and applying the content of this book.

To
the sacred Mount Govardhan,
that was instrumental in shattering the ego of
Lord Indra (who symbolizes the human senses)
with the help of the little finger of little Krishna!
In doing so, it taught humanity the lesson of
being free from the allure of the senses.

Contents

Preface	7
Part 1 Secret of Putting the Senses to Good Use	**11**
The Beginning...	13
1. The Art of Removing the Blindfold	19
2. Small Mouth Big Talk	23
3. Let the Ears Be Vigilant	27
4. Saving a Cent at the Cost of One's Skin	31
5. Not Just a Big Nose, But the Great Nose	34
6. The Art of Praying By Being Free From Desires	37
Part 2 Coaching the Senses	**41**
...Continuing...	43
7. The Confluence of the Mind and the Senses	49
8. Celibate the Senses	53
9. Develop Your Focus First, Then Attain Your Goal	57
10. Intellect Over Mind	62

11. Purifying the Mind and Senses	66
12. The Futility of Satiating the Mind and Senses	71
Part 3 Turning the Senses Inward	**75**
...Concluding	77
13. The Real Goal of the Mind and Senses	83
14. When the Self-realized Trains the Self	87
15. Whom Should the Senses Listen	91
16. Tell Your Senses "No New News"	95
17. How to Master Your Senses	100
18. The State of Liberation from the Senses	104
Appendix - The Complete Meditation of the Senses	109
Appendices	114

Preface
Reining Over Your Senses is True Success

We all are gifted with five senses of perception—eyesight, hearing, smell, taste, and touch. Imagine if there were six or seven senses, would you manage them all, or would that be out of bounds for you? Today, you can manage yourself in the world of your eyes, ears, tongue, skin, and nose with great difficulty. How, then, will you manage the new senses?

Let's try to understand the depth of this question with some suppositions. Imagine if you had a third eye on the back of your head that would enable you to see what's happening behind you. Or imagine if you could see microbes that are generally not visible to the naked eye. Or, let's say you can hear subtle infrasonic or ultrasonic sound waves. How will you manage these extra-sensory faculties? Will they be a burden on you?

Take a pause to contemplate: Do you rein over your senses, or do your senses dominate you? Do you wish you had more senses of perception, or are you happy with what you already have?

Some people may say, "We are already tormented by the illusory allure of the world. Instead of helping us achieve our goal, our senses tend to indulge and distract us further away from the goal." The illusory charm of the senses has swayed these people. But now, they want to focus on achieving their goal. So, they are busy managing their existing senses and do not aspire for new senses.

While others say, "Though it's not a necessity for us, we wouldn't mind if we were given new additional senses as we have learned to safeguard ourselves from the illusory attractions of the world. We can make use of the new senses, too, to achieve our goal. We can manage them." Such people regard whatever they receive as a blessing and make good use of them to bring all-round harmony in their lives. They lead a simple but powerful life.

Some people desire more senses, but their goal is not to safeguard themselves from the illusory world but to indulge in it even more. They say, "We want to satisfy our desires to the fullest for which any number of senses will fall short for us. Who has seen tomorrow? Let us enjoy today to the fullest." Such people are so engrossed in the illusory world that they regard fulfilling the desires arising from their senses as the sole goal of their life, whether it benefits them or not.

Which of these three answers applies to you? Or do you have a fourth answer?

Your answer determines your present state. If you want your senses to be instrumental in your success, you need to train them to work in the right direction. Let us understand this with the help of an analogy.

Some boats are sailing in a river. Imagine that you are sitting in one of them. The boat is surrounded by water on all sides. People sitting in boats around you are having fun. They are looking out through various binoculars attached to their boats and enjoying their journey. There are five different types of binoculars fitted to your boat too. Out of curiosity, you also start looking out through them. Scenes that were far away now seem closer.

You enjoy the sight of the lush green, flower-laden trees through one of the binoculars. You see wild animals in the mountains through another binocular and get horrified. They appear so close to you as if they will pounce on you anytime. Thus, you enjoy, become stressed, feel anxious, or afraid while looking through the different binoculars.

The boat also has a big switch that controls all the binoculars, but you don't have complete knowledge about it. You get engrossed in what you see through the binoculars and forget that you are on a journey.

In this analogy, the boat you boarded is your body, and the five binoculars are your senses—eyes, nose, ears, tongue, and skin. The water around the boat is the web of illusory attractions surrounding you.

You have come to Earth with your body and mind, and are bestowed with the five binoculars to aid you in your journey. By using them, you can sense and overcome the obstacles in your way and safely reach your ultimate destination. The big switch is your mind. Since you are unaware of how your mind works, you are unable to use it properly. You use it the same way others do.

A wise one does not fall into the trap of the illusory world. Instead, he makes his trained senses and mind instrumental in achieving the ultimate goal of his life. Those whose senses and mind are untrained remain trapped in the illusory world. Their senses are always engrossed in the world. They see that everyone around them does the same, so they imitate them without giving much thought. This hinders their journey towards their goal, and they lead a distressed life.

If you want to complete your life's journey with ease, simplicity, and happiness, you must train and conquer your mind and senses. This book serves as a guide to coach your mind and senses. It helps you to empower them so that you can achieve complete success in life because reining over your senses amounts to achieving success in life. After all, understanding the inner secrets within you can help you achieve outer success.

PART 1
Secret of Putting the Senses to Good Use

The Beginning...

Lord Indra's royal court was luxuriously embellished. Beautiful paintings adorned the walls. Magnificent chandeliers decked the dome and ceiling. Gods and Goddesses were seated on plush chairs on both sides. The grandeur of the royal court was an impressive sight to behold.

Nineteen-year-old Devesh jumped with joy on seeing all this in the TV serial. "Great! What an idea! Let's surprise mom and dad by using this theme for their twenty-fifth wedding anniversary celebration!"

For a long time, Devesh was on the lookout for a theme for this party, which presented itself in this TV serial. He felt that it was just the most suitable theme for their party. Without wasting time, he reached out to a decorator and explained the fine details of the royal palace theme with its elegant decorations.

He invited the elders of his family, cousins, neighbors, and acquaintances to the party to witness the royal theme of Lord Indra's court. He eagerly awaited that day.

Soon, the day arrived. His Grandpa also came down from their native town along with other relatives. Devesh's joy knew no bounds on seeing him as he dearly loved his Grandpa. All the guests were wonderstruck on seeing the spectacular decoration. The splendor of the palatial décor, the ambiance of colorful lights, and the paintings on the walls were captivating. The melodious music, the alluring aroma of delectable dishes, and the enchanting fragrance of flowers enriched the atmosphere. His parents were also delighted by this pleasant surprise.

The party ended at the planned hour. Everyone was thrilled when they returned home. Devesh's parents praised him, which made him feel proud. When Devesh escorted his Grandpa to his room, he curiously asked him, "Grandpa, how did you find the party?"

Grandpa smiled, "The party was indeed great! You left no stone unturned to entertain the guests. The decoration was too good, and the food was undoubtedly delicious. Even the servants were pleased with the way you had made all the arrangements."

Devesh asked in surprise, "But, there were only relatives and dad's colleagues at the party. Which servants are you talking about?"

Grandpa got to bed, leaving his question unanswered. Devesh felt that Grandpa might be tired, feeling sleepy. He didn't notice Grandpa's enigmatic smile. He kept wondering, "Which servants was Grandpa talking about? I didn't see any!" Deeply engrossed in his thoughts, he didn't realize when he fell asleep.

As soon as he woke up the next morning, he remembered Grandpa's words. He quickly finished his morning chores and rushed to meet Grandpa. He was having tea, sitting in the balcony. Devesh seized the opportunity and asked, "Grandpa, which servants were you talking about last night? I didn't see any servant." Grandpa wittily replied, "Isn't it time for you to go to college? We can discuss this in the evening." As Devesh turned to go, Grandpa merrily remarked, "I will be staying on for a few more days." Devesh was thrilled to hear this. He, too, had wished that Grandpa should stay with them for a few more days. He happily left for his college, promising to meet Grandpa in the evening.

* * *

When Devesh finished his classroom sessions, he returned home instead of hanging out with his friends. As he reached home, Grandpa was setting out for a stroll. Devesh quickly freshened up and accompanied him.

When they reached a nearby garden, Grandpa asked, "So, how was your day?"

"It was great, Grandpa! We had a lot of fun. During the recess, I had some spicy snacks with my friends in the canteen, listened to some music, and chit-chatted about yesterday's party."

"And what about your studies?"

Devesh's excitement sank, "Yes, we attended some lectures."

"Hmm, how much do you score in the exams?"

"Earlier, I used to be good at studies, but nowadays, I find it difficult to concentrate on my studies. That's why I've not been scoring too well these days."

"Okay, have you tried to find the root cause?"

Devesh looked perplexed, "Umm, no, I haven't. But I'm trying hard to study well."

"Would you like to know about it?"

"If it's going to improve my grades, I'd like to know for sure."

"Then know for sure that it's all related to your six senses."

"But Grandpa, we have only five senses, right?"

"Yes, but our mind is also associated with our senses. So, they are six. Let's talk about the five senses first. Our five senses entangle us in the attractions of the world. For example, instead of focusing on your studies, your eyes pull you towards captivating sights. You enjoy watching movies, binge-watching Netflix shows for hours together. Your ears get engrossed in listening to music instead of lectures. Your tongue likes to relish a variety of delicious food. In short, each of your senses compels you to fulfill their desires and pulls you away from your studies."

Devesh pondered and then said, "You're right. That's exactly what's happening these days. I tend to be lost in what my senses compel me to do. Though I also want to study, I feel drawn towards these pleasures."

"It only means that you're not clear about your goal. At present, you need to prioritize your studies over everything else to achieve success and steer your life in the right direction. But you forget this and get deluded by your senses, thus drifting away from your chosen path. Your senses have become your master. You oblige by fulfilling their demands, and instead of being their master, you become a servant to them."

"Oh! Now I get it. Is that why you said last night that all the servants were satisfied?"

"Yes, because the senses that are gifted to us are our servants. They should be obliging us, but these days the reverse is happening. We have fallen prey to them and keep trying to please them!"

"Grandpa, you must be tired of walking. Why don't we sit for a while?"

Both sat on a bench in the park.

They noticed some people practicing yoga on a platform in the middle of the ground in front. After finishing yoga, some of them enjoyed fried savories at the roadside carts. Some were busy taking pictures in the park. They also saw a blind man entering the park with his stick. He walked around the park and then calmly sat on a bench.

"What do you think about the senses after seeing this? Are they a boon or a curse to us?"

Devesh mused for a while and then replied, "Of course, they are a boon, Grandpa! What is life without them? That blind gentleman must be finding it so difficult without eyesight. We can easily perform our daily chores as we are blessed with eyesight."

"You're right! But have you seen a blind man with eyesight?"

Devesh was surprised, "A blind man with eyes?!"

"Yes! Look at that other man. He has come here for a walk to make his health, but his eyes are glued to the food carts. He is satiating the craving of his taste buds at the cost of tormenting his poor stomach. Despite having eyes, he cannot see that the street food on the food carts is pulling him away from his resolve to improve his health. He has become servile to the demands of his taste buds. Wouldn't you call him a blind man with eyesight? The way we use our senses determines whether they are a boon or a curse for us. If you're able to use them properly, they can help you achieve your goal and remain successful."

"Grandpa, you are right! I want to learn more about this. For the last few days, I have been feeling guilty about deviating from my studies and my goal of having a progressive career in a multinational organization. I have wasted crucial time watching TV, being stuck to my mobile phone, watching movies, and partying with my friends. But now I want to progress in my life. Your coming here is godsent as I'm now getting to know these things from you."

"I'm glad that you're keen to know about this. Now you can regain your focus on your goal by making your senses a blessing."

"But Grandpa, how do our senses become so powerful that they entangle us? How can we gain control over them?"

Grandpa looked at his watch, "Well… it's getting late. Let's go home. We can continue this discussion tomorrow. Can you do some homework till then?"

Devesh smiled, "Sure, I'll complete your assignment along with my coursework."

"Alright. So, until we meet tomorrow, contemplate how you should listen to your senses. When do the senses turn into a curse?

For example, if your eyes constantly crave to watch your favorite film stars, movies, or web series, they become a curse. Likewise, contemplate each of the senses and write in your diary. Does this work?"

"Yes, Grandpa! I surely will."

Devesh and Grandpa walked back home.

To be continued on page 45

1

The Art of Removing the Blindfold

"Mom, I have a business meeting in the morning. If all goes well, I will bag a huge order, and this should also put an end to all our money problems," Vikas told his mother as he was getting ready to leave.

"Okay son. But be sure that you make it on time."

"Yes, mom, I'll be there on time." He thought, "Since I've got five more minutes to leave, let me munch on some snack." He took some cookies in a bowl and started munching them. As he reached the living room, he saw his dad watching the climax of a suspense film. Curious to know the outcome, he sat down on a sofa next to his dad. While the minutes ticked, he got engrossed as the suspense scene of the film unfolded.

When the film was over, he realized he had spent fifteen minutes watching the film. He hastily finished his other tasks and left. By the time he reached the meeting venue, it was too late. He appealed for the next appointment but couldn't get it. Feeling deeply remorseful for not having made it to the meeting on time, he sat in the lounge with his face buried in his hands.

We can see how Vikas lost a golden opportunity by being swayed by visual enticements. Sometimes, even a delay of ten to fifteen minutes can prove disastrous. This also happens to many of us. We often get stuck in alluring sights, much against our will. As a result, our eyes get veiled by the shroud of illusion, and we stray away from our goal.

You would have noticed that children are lured by the latest web series, fashion channels, and YouTube videos nowadays. They focus on the attire, body language, and behavior of models, actors, and celebrities and try to imitate them. As a result, they forget about their studies and waste their crucial time, money, and effort.

Likewise, some people enjoy shopping. They set out to buy necessities but get carried away by the attractive items put on display. They end up buying things they will never need at the cost of omitting the essentials. They then waste time in vain, regretting wasting their time, money, and energy on futilities.

Our eyes are habituated to getting caught up in fascinating sights. Some people indulge in watching cricket matches or stock market tickers during their office hours to such an extent that they lose sight of their work.

People often get stuck on the social media, OTT entertainment services, and online shopping portals and remain bereft of the real purpose of their life. This does not mean that you should refrain from watching TV or turn a blind eye to the world. You need to ensure that it does not develop into a habit or a tendency because tendencies are the root cause of drifting away from the goal. Always keep your goal in mind while indulging your eyes.

For this, you need to remove the blindfold of illusion from your eyes and make it a boon instead of a curse. You get three opportunities to save yourself from getting caught up in a scene—before entering it, while you are in it, and after coming out of it. You may think, "What's the use of realizing after getting stuck in it?" But you can save yourself from getting stuck in the same scene the next time. Let us understand how we can make use of these three opportunities.

1. The first opportunity: If you know that you get stuck in a particular scene, prepare yourself before entering it. For example, suppose you know that you tend to get absorbed in the social media or surfing the internet. Before connecting to the social media or the internet, recall your goal, and decide your time limit. This will help you focus on the time spent and remind you of your goal.

2. The second opportunity: If you get stuck in a scene and suddenly realize it, immediately become aware. You may have heard many times that our eyes work exactly like a TV screen. We remember some things that we have seen but forget many things we have heard. Hence, we must be vigilant about the scenes we capture through our eyes. If you get caught up in certain scenes, associate the importance of your goal with them so that those scenes can remind you of your goal or prod you to achieve your goal. Also, ask yourself, "Is this scene reminding me of my goal, or am I getting caught up in it and deviating from my goal?"

3. The third opportunity: When you get caught up in a scene and realize your mistake only after coming out of it, contemplate, "What was my lesson in that scene, and what will I do when the scene recurs?" Decide after contemplating and stick to it.

You would have observed a bee getting fascinated by the beauty of a lotus flower. It sits on a fully bloomed lotus in the morning and does not realize when it's dusk. When the lotus closes its petals in the evening, the bee gets trapped inside and dies. In contrast, a honeybee sits on several flowers and flies away after sucking the nectar because it is aware of its goal. It focuses on making honey instead of getting entangled in flowers.

Therefore, reflect on your life: Which scenes fascinate and distract you from your goal. This reflection will help you focus more on your goal and be less drawn toward the deluding scenes. For this, pay attention to the following points.

- Befriend your eyes by watching only purposeful programs from a plethora of programs broadcast through various channels. Don't keep watching programs on TV or OTT platforms aimlessly. Instead, set a specific time and a time limit to watch some of your chosen programs and stick to them.

- Look at every incident and its facts positively. Prioritize maintaining your awareness during negative incidents.

- Use technology to carry out important tasks and achieve your goal instead of misusing it to watch meaningless pictures with restless eyes.

- Don't waste time reading meaningless articles, columns, and blogs from newspapers, magazines, and the social media. Instead, use that time for a more practical and relevant purpose.

- Focus on the knowledge, qualities, and achievements of others instead of their physical stature, wealth, and weaknesses.

- In every incident, focus on the strengths of others rather than their shortcomings.

- Display pictures of successful people and distinguished personalities in your study room and kitchen, which will be a source of inspiration.

- Do not indulge in wild daydreaming. It is like building a castle in the air. Craving for the gratification of sensory desires never gives true fulfillment.

2

Small Mouth Big Talk

Nowadays, multi-cuisine restaurants have become commonplace. Many of them serve a variety of delicacies from various regions of the world. We can relish a variety of dishes from different states of India as well as Oriental, Italian, Mexican, or Mediterranean cuisines. These restaurants are increasingly becoming the go-to preference for people who throng them—without discernment.

The new wave of addiction that all this has brought about is unprecedented. The problem is not about the quality of food on offer but the addictive mindset that develops over time. It is as if people live to eat rather than eat to live. People get together to discuss options to satisfy their palate. They plan to visit new restaurants and try new cuisines every time. Both children and adults have fallen prey to the lure of the taste buds. Many of them do not realize how this is detrimental to their health.

Therefore, introspect whether you are also meddling with your health in this way? Is your tongue creating complications in your life?

Although seemingly small, our mouth holds a powerful tool that can make or break our life. Our tongue may appear diminutive and yet wields the power to rule the world. Hence, it is apt to say "small-mouth big-talk." While the tongue rules the external world through the power of speech, it rules our inner world through the power of its taste buds!

The tongue is a flexible and delicate sense organ that can either render us good health or spoil our health depending on the kind of food it demands.

Let us understand how taste affects our health. The tongue is indeed nature's gift that we are blessed with to experience different flavors. The primary purpose of the tongue is to act as a gatekeeper to deny passage to food that could be harmful to our body and permit only healthy food. But, today, we are so caught up in the variety of tastes that we invite several illnesses due to inappropriate food intake. These days it has become a trend to eat more than our real hunger demands, pamper the taste buds with sugary sweets despite being diabetic, gobble food hurriedly, or have junk food due to our busy and fast lifestyle.

As we are unaware of where this passion for food is leading us, our body is falling victim to various illnesses day by day. It is time to safeguard us from this food trap. Let's understand some remedies for this.

- Eat only when you are really hungry. Eating by the clock without appetite leads to malnutrition. Our body doesn't absorb essential nutrients from the food due to the lack of adequate digestive juices secreted by the taste glands and digestive system.

- Always eat a little less than your appetite. By overeating, our body becomes lethargic. Excessive food gets stored in the body in the form of fat which causes obesity and diseases.

- Use a simple, small, yet powerful technique whenever you feel like having something you are not supposed to have. Suppose you relish sweets, but their excessive intake is detrimental to your health. Then instead of restraining yourself from having it, have it and leave a small portion of it behind. Tell yourself, "Although I love this sweet, as it does not align with my health goals, I would rather leave it." This clearly indicates your subconscious mind that you want to get rid of this habit. Gradually, your subconscious mind gets convinced about it and acts upon it. Thus, you become free from it.

On a different note, tongue forms the basis of our relationships through the words we utter. It can either foster harmonious relations by wielding sweet words that can please and reassure people or damage relations within seconds by flinging sharp, bitter words at people. Because of its exploits, it is commonly regarded by several names like foodie palate, a double-edged sword, or a talking scissor.

As for the words uttered by the tongue, we need to be wary about our words. Every word that we speak is important. Sweet words build trust in relationships, while bitter words create distrust and bitterness in people's hearts.

Contemplate, "When do you speak bitter words that affect your relationships?" Some people are habituated to lying or using abusive words. Over time, it becomes their nature. Some people are habituated to speaking all the time harshly. Later, it becomes their way of conversing. When asked, they say, "This is my normal tone," but it profoundly affects their relationships.

These days, most people lead a stressful life due to their hectic lifestyle. The sweetness of speech seems to disappear. There is so much tension in families that, let alone sweet words, people are engaged in belittling others with their words or hurling hurtful words at them. As words lose their value due to their hollow usage, people stop trusting each other.

Even if they want to share their heartfelt feelings with others, they cannot do so. For example, if they wish to tell someone, "I'm your well-wisher. I care for you. You must read this book. It's essential for you," they simply say, "That's fine. It's okay. No problem." Although they have sweet words on their tongue, they find it difficult to use them due to a lack of habit or reluctance.

When you value the worth of your words, you can bring about a transformation in your life. To imbibe the habit of using sweet words, you must speak a new positive word daily and repeat it whenever you remember during the day. You can find abundant sweet words and phrases in a dictionary, which you can indeed include in your everyday language.

For example, you can say, "I have great respect for you. I feel inspired by you. You are competent. I am proud of you. I like you. I love your company." People love to hear such words.

"Please," "Sorry," and "Thank you" are golden words, provided they are spoken from the heart. We should make them a part of our life. We should teach their importance to children from an early age. Children will then automatically start using them from the heart. As you begin using sweet words that you would like to hear in your conversation, it will bring sweetness to your life and relationships.

3

Let the Ears Be Vigilant

"The music is melodious."

"Your words sound like music to my ears."

"Early in the morning, we feel sacred and serene while listening to the ringing of the temple bells."

You may have often heard such statements. We hear all kinds of sounds, be it the chirping of birds, the seven tones of music, the whizzing of a breeze, the rumble of the waves, the rustle of leaves, the sound of laughter and banter between friends, or a heated argument between people.

Like the eyes, our ears also serve as a highway for drawing information from the outside world. Whatever we hear directly affects our mind. It is scientifically proven that sweet, pleasing words filled with love positively affect not just human beings but flora and fauna too. On the other hand, immature listeners can ruin their life by merely listening to demoralizing and ridiculing words about them.

The ears are so powerful that they become active right from the time the baby is in the womb. You may be aware of the story of Abhimanyu in the Indian epic Mahabharata. He had heard about the creation of the *Chakravyuha* (a labyrinthian military layout) when he was in his mother's womb. Hence, it is said that a pregnant woman should listen to sweet words, soothing music and perform noble activities during her pregnancy so that the child can imbibe good values.

We connect with the outside world primarily through our ears and eyes. The eyes get caught up in the sights, while the ears believe whatever they hear directly or indirectly and hold on to it for a lifetime.

For example, a mother scolds her child, "You are good for nothing; you cannot do a single task properly." Such words get deeply ingrained in his subconscious mind. Even after growing up, when he takes up some work, he is reminded of those words and loses confidence. Similarly, people remember words like, "You are short," "You are dark," "You are unworthy" for their lifetime. At times, such words stay with them for their lifetime, hindering their self-esteem and success.

Hence, before listening to others' words and believing them to be true, first contemplate on them and cautiously choose whether to believe in them. This is how you become a mature listener. Otherwise, our mind can get contaminated by the meaningless hearsay of people. Sometimes, even a trivial talk can change the course of our life.

You may know Manthara, the spiteful character in the Indian epic Ramayana. She persuaded Queen Kaikeyi to ask for the two boons promised to her by King Dasharatha. Although Kaikeyi was a thoughtful, mature, and affectionate mother, she fell prey to Manthara's words and thus changed the course of her thoughts. Believing in the venomous words of Manthara, she asked the king to banish Lord Rama on a fourteen-year exile and proclaim her son Bharat as the heir to the throne.

There was only one Manthara in the Ramayana. But today, we get to see many Mantharas in different forms at every step as follows -

- Manthara in the form of advertisements: People listen to advertisements on TV over and over again, such as "This soap, this lotion will enhance your beauty; this biscuit, juice, or vitamin supplement will boost your child's strength," and so on. When someone tells them about a sale with a super discount on certain products, they rush to avail the benefits without considering their utility.

- Manthara in the form of the social media: Many people waste hours listening to funny stories on the social media platforms, besides listening to news channels.

- Manthara that can mislead us in crooked ways: Some people get their not-so-simple jobs done by others by resorting to deceit or threatening them.

In the Ramayana, Lord Rama was exiled because of Manthara. But today's Manthara affects our lives in two ways -

Firstly, she programs our subconscious mind negatively, the consequences of which are seen later. For example, whenever you see or hear some negative news, you unknowingly attract similar incidents in your life. By thinking, "This shouldn't happen to me" or "If this happens to me, I'll react like this," you inadvertently attract those incidents in your life.

Therefore, contemplate: How many types of Mantharas are present in your life that make inroads into your subconscious mind? Understand them and safeguard yourself from them.

From today onwards, whenever you hear such negative news or watch a TV serial, fold your hands, or make three crosses with your hand (X X X) or say, "Cancel, cancel, cancel." This will clearly signal to your subconscious mind that you don't want these events in your life. It won't record these incidents or accept them as the truth.

The second type of Manthara spoils relationships by bickering in the family. Find them. For example, some people waste time in chit-chat or gossiping out of habit. Sometimes, they create rifts in families by back-biting one another. They enjoy gossiping about a third person who is absent or spreading rumors about them. These are their favorite pastimes. People don't care about their relationships when they indulge in such second-rate entertainment.

Whenever this type of Manthara tries to seduce and mislead you, ask yourself, "Is whatever I am hearing the complete truth?"

As soon as you raise this question, you start reflecting on it and can become aware of the reality, "Maybe this is a partial truth. What I believe could be a misunderstanding, and the truth could be quite the opposite."

Trust is another powerful tool that can help you ignore Manthara. When there is love and trust in the family, no outsider can instigate quarrels.

Besides this, learn the art of listening. Give more importance to listening rather than talking. It is observed that everyone has a strong urge to speak. Wherever they go, they wish, "I should speak, and others should listen to me." They often interrupt others' conversations. This tendency to predominantly talk makes them poor listeners, and they fail to understand what others have to say.

To safeguard yourself from the harmful effects of Manthara's words, listen completely with awareness only to the truth.

4

Saving a Cent at the Cost of One's Skin

A mother's touch is a pleasant feeling. Words fall short of expressing this experience. Whether a human child or bird or animal, it first experiences its mother's warm and reassuring touch at its birth and always cherishes that touch throughout its life. It feels secure when it basks in that touch.

As the child grows up, he starts perceiving objects by touch. He finds some sensations pleasant and some others unpleasant. For example, he dislikes touching some hard or thorny objects. Whereas, he likes hugging some people, shaking hands with them, being patted on his back and patting others, etc., as he experiences love through such touch.

We have sensory receptors below our skin, which help us become aware of every touch or sensation. Sensations can't be seen but can only be felt. For example, we perceive an itching sensation or hot or cold feeling due to our skin's sensitivity.

Whenever the skin comes in contact with any object, the sensory receptors make us aware of it. The perceptive faculty of the mind determines whether the touch is soothing or irritating. Whenever we touch a soft or a cold thing, we feel good about it. Whereas, we feel painful when we touch some hot object or a wound on the body.

Thus, everyone tries to avoid unpleasant touch experiences, such as the feeling of sweat during summer, the painful feeling experienced in the body during aches, pricking of an object, etc. These sensations make one restless and distracted.

They get attached to pleasant sensations and wish to experience them repeatedly. They even get into some bad habits to repeat the pleasant experiences. For example, if someone likes the comfortable feeling of an easy chair or a bean bag, he spends hours sitting on it doing nothing. If someone feels like scratching, he repeatedly keeps scratching at the itchy spot.

He often spends his money on getting the comforts that merely give a soothing experience to the skin. For him, the phrase "Save A Cent at the Cost of One's Skin" is exactly the opposite because he is ready to pay a high price for a good experience of touch.

However, the sensations of touch on the skin, be it good or bad, do not last for long. They remain for some time and then vanish. Still, one gets so attached to them that he tries to avoid the unpleasant sensations and hanker after pleasant ones.

Contemplate for some time: "What kind of sensations do you get stuck in? What kind of sensations do you hanker after repeatedly, and what kind of sensations do you avoid?"

If you carefully observe, one's mental state affects the kind of sensations one has. For example, if one keeps repeating during summer, "It's too hot these days," he will tend to feel a more profuse sweating sensation on his body. Suppose he is fearful, in a dilemma or excited, he experiences goosebumps on his body, his heartbeat races, and he experiences a strange sensation on his body. It happens with everyone sometime or the other. On the contrary, when he meditates or prays, that too affects his body. When the mind completely calms down, he experiences positive energy vibrating in every cell, every part of his body.

When you start observing every sensation attentively during meditation, your mental state changes. Sometimes, it becomes difficult to calm the mind, drive away fearful thoughts, or put aside worries. It is helpful to watch these sensations arising from such emotions. Sometimes, you fail to figure out the mental state that causes a particular sensation in the body. As you dislike that sensation, it aggravates the mental state further.

There is not a single moment during a day when you don't have a sensation. Attentively work on the sensations you get stuck with more often. For example, many people dislike the sensation caused due to confrontation with the crowd while traveling by public transport. It makes them fume with anger. At the same time, others keep their calm amid the crowd. This is possible because they playfully observe the complete situation from a detached standpoint. When their destination arrives, they alight peacefully.

Practice following meditation to observe every sensation attentively from a detached standpoint instead of being attached to it, hankering after it, or avoiding it. First, read the steps, understand them, and then practice it.

1. Close your eyes and sit in a meditative posture.
2. Attentively observe the sensations arising in your body.
3. Whenever any sensation arises, observe how deep it penetrates your skin. With awareness, you will know that it is felt only on the surface of your skin and not deep within.
4. Further, observe how long that sensation lasts and when it subsides. As it resides only at the superficial level, it lasts for some time. It is temporary. If you watch the sensation from a detached standpoint without giving it undue importance, it does not trouble you much and subsides on its own after some time.
5. In this manner, repeat the above mentioned steps for every sensation. As you observe every sensation with detachment without getting stuck to it, all associated emotions dissolve and your mental state becomes stable and positive.

5

Not Just a Big Nose, But the Great Nose

The first drizzle of the monsoon rains! The earthy fragrance! There is hardly anyone who is not familiar with it. When we visit a hill station, the pure and fresh air in the open environment rejuvenates our body completely. Besides the whiff of the leaves, a waft of breeze brings a sweet fragrance of fresh flowers and soaks our sense of smell. As the nose smells the fragrance, we feel refreshed. This is the magic of the sense of smell. Whether it is a fragrance or a stink, whether we like it or not, we get to smell it.

Yes, we are talking about the nose, which allows us to experience the sense of smell. Whether an animal or a human being, the nose takes care of the vital functions of smelling and breathing.

Smelling - the first purpose of the nose

There is always some smell in the air. Our nose makes us aware of it. When we breathe, we sense this smell mixed in the air. Our mind feels pleasant on smelling a fragrance, but it tries to get away from a foul smell.

Animals have such an acute sense of smell that they sense danger and protect themselves just by sniffing. They pre-empt any unpleasant event or calamities like floods, earthquakes, or storms in advance and flee. Humans also have a strong sense of smell, but its ability diminishes as it gets contaminated with time.

This contamination happens because of our habit of classifying odors as good or bad. Markets are flooded with products to safeguard us from foul odor, such as room fresheners, car fresheners, mouth fresheners, scented incense sticks, spices, etc.

There are so many fragrances available today that fake fragrances have started trending more than natural ones. The demand for perfumes and deodorants has increased to satisfy the sense of smell. Even materials used for worship are made available with artificial fragrance, due to which its original odor is lost.

Today, we have become so used to scented material that we cannot stand even the slightest stink. Due to this, disorders and diseases like anger, irritability, allergies, nausea, and anxiety have increased.

Breathing - the second purpose of the nose

A blind person can live without seeing. The deaf can also survive without hearing. One can survive for a long time without having delicious food. Even the dumb can lead their life, albeit with some inconvenience. Even if someone has rashes on their skin, they survive. But one cannot live without breathing. Life force is needed to keep the physical body alive. Hence, the nose is one of the most important gifts bestowed on human beings.

The process of inhaling and exhaling goes on continuously. However, we pay no heed to whether we are breathing fresh air. Those who stay confined to air-conditioned rooms for the whole day do not get to breathe pure fresh air. They are unaware that their bodies slowly become home to many diseases as they constantly breathe recycled air in closed rooms. As a result, these days, even children suffer from breathing problems like asthma, nervousness, headache, etc. Nowadays, the youth are also complaining of joint pains.

We should consider these ailments as a warning bell to improve our health. It is necessary to take some time out from our routine to practice Pranayama and go for daily walks. At the same time, start observing our emotions along with our breathing to achieve complete physical and mental health.

Our emotions are linked to our breathing. As our emotions change, so does our breathing pattern. When we are scared or angry, we tend to breathe rapidly. When we are relaxed, we breathe slowly. When we are full of hatred, greed, or restlessness, our breath tends to be shallow or intermittently rapid. We breathe differently at various times of the day. Sometimes the air passes through both the nostrils and sometimes through only one nostril. This keeps changing. Even the slightest change in our mental state affects our breathing.

From today, observe the pace and rhythm of your breathing. Try to understand how your emotions affect the way you breathe and how your breathing rate changes from time to time.

When we are overwhelmed with negative thoughts or we start breathing rapidly, we need to gauge our breathing pattern first and then start counting in the reverse order from 100. With this, we will regain control over our breath, and negative emotions also gradually begin to subside. For example, if we are experiencing exam fear or stage fear, we should take at least three long, deep breaths and exhale slowly. As soon as we begin to watch our emotions with alertness, we feel better because our breath has a close connection with our thoughts and feelings.

You can also try an experiment with your breath for better health. Hold your mouth puffed up like Hanuman from the Ramayana. Keep inhaling the air and fill your mouth till it is puffed up. Then slowly let go of the air from your mouth. Repeat this one more time. Holding the air in your mouth, inhale and exhale slowly through your nose, then release it. In the process, you will experience strength in your tongue and mouth.

Regard every breath as a blessing and enjoy it. Inculcate the habit of observing and counting your breaths. This will make you aware of the slightest changes in your emotions and increase your awareness. When you continue to watch your breath, emotions begin to lose their momentum.

6

The Art of Praying By Being Free From Desires

Everyone knows about the practice of fasting by going without food or on a reduced diet. The healthy practice of fasting gives intermittent rest to our stomach and intestines so that our digestive system gets rejuvenated and works smoothly.

But have you ever heard of fasting of the senses? Fasting of the senses implies abstaining from sensory indulgence. Very few or almost none are aware of such abstinence.

Our senses play an important role in completing our daily tasks, and they work continuously without a break. They are a boon bestowed on us, but when they become a curse and cause us misery, it becomes necessary to control them so that they work in our favor.

If we consciously abstain from indulging in our senses for even a day and focus them in the right direction, they can help us progress towards our goal.

Have you ever asked yourself, "How much do my senses help me achieve my goal? Do I thoughtlessly lead life by indulging my senses indiscriminately?"

Whether the goal is big or small, everyone strives hard to achieve it. They succeed in being on track for some time, but then their senses get the better of them. They get trapped in the web of their senses and go astray from their life's goal. To avoid this mistake, exercise control over your senses. This is possible only when you impart the right training to your senses.

We have already mentioned a few techniques to control the senses in the earlier chapters. Here, we will learn about one more technique for abstaining from the senses.

When we fast, we refrain from eating or drinking for some time or even for the entire day. We exercise control over our sense of taste and bear with hunger pangs. However, when we abstain from our senses, we should stop using one of the senses for some time—for a few hours or a few minutes—or at least use it with awareness. We can also opt for doing something positive in that sense.

We may find this difficult initially as our mind will try to avoid it. The mind is habituated to indulge in sensory content. It does not let any sense remain at peace without sensory content. It starts planning the next activity even before the earlier or ongoing activity finishes. Now, we need to persuade and train this mind to sit in silence for some time. Let us understand with some examples how we can practice abstaining each of the senses for some minutes or hours on a particular day. You can choose some options from the list below or create your options.

Options for abstaining from the eyes:

1. Today, I will not watch TV for a chosen hour or the entire day. Or I shall not watch my favorite TV serial or web series.
2. Today, I will stay away from my mobile for half an hour or not use the Social Media app for an hour.
3. Today, I will read a chapter from my favorite book.
4. Today, I will not pay attention to anyone's vices.
5. Today, I will close my eyes and meditate or contemplate for some time.

Options for abstaining from the ears:

1. Today, I will not give undue importance to anyone's harsh words.
2. Today, I will not listen to any unproductive criticism at home, office, or community about people, politicians, and others.
3. Today, I will listen to some light music, devotional songs, or motivational talk for an hour.
4. Today, I will not listen to any loud music. I will watch TV at a low volume.
5. Today, I will listen to discourses on the truth for an hour.

Options for abstaining from the tongue:

1. I will not eat junk food or dine out for the next month.
2. Today, I shall not satiate my hunger completely. I shall have less food than what my hunger demands. I will not overeat.
3. Today, I shall have one meal without salt and with lesser spices.
4. Today, I shall not talk ill about those who are not present, or I shall not indulge in bickering or backbiting.
5. Today, I shall use sweet words like "Thank you" and "Sorry."
6. Today, I shall speak in a soft tone.

Options for abstaining from the sense of smell:

1. Today, I will not use my favorite perfume.
2. Today, I shall work on my health by practicing Pranayama for half an hour.
3. Today, I shall breathe deeply for a minute every hour.
4. Today, I shall observe my emotions along with my breath while I am at my workplace.

5. Today, I will make the atmosphere pleasant and happy by lighting incense sticks at home.

Options for abstaining from the sense of touch:

1. Today, I will keep myself away from soothing or soft touch. For example, I am used to sleeping on my bed, perhaps a soft mattress. I will experiment sleeping on another mattress for a night, maybe a hard one.
2. I will observe every touch sensation for an hour. It could be a soft touch, a rough touch, an itching sensation, etc.
3. Today, I will observe all sensations with closed eyes without reacting for some time. For example, how long can I experience the sensations of pain, itch, or pricking while sitting quietly.
4. Today, I will watch every emotion in response to various sensations with awareness. For example, the feeling of love with a hug, irritability with sweat during summer, etc.

Thus, we can resolve to abstain from our senses to exercise control over them to achieve our desired goals.

PART 2
Coaching the Senses

...Continuing...

Devesh completed the contemplation homework assigned by his Grandpa. He started noticing how his senses were becoming a curse rather than a boon to him throughout the day. He began to like the newfound awareness and understanding of his senses. He was eager to share this with his Grandpa.

When he met Grandpa in the evening, he was sitting in the balcony, enjoying tea. The weather was pleasant, as if it would rain at any time. After some idle talk, Grandpa enquired with Devesh about the homework he had assigned. Devesh enthusiastically shared his new insights about the senses and posed a few questions to him: "Is it wrong to have desires? Do we need to suppress our desires to turn them into blessings? Don't desires drive us to move forward? How can one function in life in the absence of desires?"

Seeing his anxiety and eagerness, Grandpa replied, "Stop the flurry of questions! It's not wrong to have desires, but it is wrong to get trapped in them and deviate from your goal. These days, most youngsters assume gratifying their mind and senses as the sole goal of life. Hence, they live a life of indulgence. Let's discuss the desires aroused by the senses today. We are always intent on gratifying our senses. And for this, we keep satisfying Lord Indra - the Lord of senses!

"In Indian mythology, Lord Indra symbolizes the human senses. You would have read stories or watched TV serials where Lord Indra is depicted as the egoistic king of the gods, enjoying the lavish lifestyle in the heavenly realm. Often, he is taught a lesson so that he stays within his limits. For example, once his ego was shattered by the sacred Mount Govardhan with the help of little Lord Krishna."

Devesh was curious, "Grandpa… What was the story? I don't remember."

Grandpa narrated the story. "Once, the residents of Braj (the village where Lord Krishna spent his childhood) were preparing for the annual rituals to worship Lord Indra. Based on each one's capacity, they all were doing their best to offer foodstuff and prepare dishes for the ritual.

"Little Krishna asked his mother Yashoda, 'Whom are you all preparing to worship?' Yashoda replied, 'Lord Indra. We do this every year because it is by his mercy that we get sufficient rainfall and abundant crop produce for ourselves and our cattle.'

"Hearing this, Lord Krishna said, 'If you have to worship anyone at all, then worship Mount Govardhan, not Lord Indra. It is his fundamental duty to shower rain. So, worship Mount Govardhan as it feeds our cattle with lush green grass, due to which we get milk, curd, and butter. The pure water flowing from this mountain is the lifeline for our village. We also get various medicinal herbs from the mountain. It satisfies all our essential needs. Hence, we should rather worship Mount Govardhan.'

"All the villagers of Braj were touched by little Krishna's words and decided to worship Mount Govardhan instead of Lord Indra. Angered by this, Lord Indra vented his wrath by flooding the village with torrential rain. As the heavy rains flooded the village, the villagers started cursing little Krishna. Then, Krishna lifted Mount Govardhan with his little finger to save the residents from the deluge. All the villagers and their cattle remained safe under the mountain for seven days. This magnanimous act agitated Lord Indra and shattered his ego."

Devesh asked Grandpa, "So, this also means that everyone was saved because of Mount Govardhan, right?"

Grandpa replied, "That's right. Lord Krishna asked people to worship Mount Govardhan to make them understand its importance. Mount Govardhan symbolizes tolerance, willpower, patience, and resoluteness. By resting on the little finger of little Krishna, it shattered the ego of Lord Indra, who represents restlessness, arrogance, and the endless craving for sensory pleasures and appreciation.

"Like Lord Indra, our senses, too, become arrogant. When all their wishes are gratified, they make more demands. It is like pouring oil into an insatiable fire. Hence, we should be firm, determined, and patient like Mount Govardhan so that we, too, can direct our senses towards our goal.

"Stories from the *Puranas* usually depict how the throne of Lord Indra trembles at the slightest challenge to his ego. A trembling seat signifies indulging the senses, feeling challenged and threatened. If we have not set our goal, we can easily get trapped in the vicious cycle of the senses."

Devesh agreed and said, "You're right, Grandpa. When we are not clear about our goal, we get trapped in the senses. Hence, I have been thinking about my goal since yesterday. I want to reach the pinnacle of success in my career."

Grandpa explained, "Everyone wants to be successful in their life, but they need to choose the right path and work hard for that. You asked me yesterday why the senses are so powerful. It's because of the mind."

Devesh was surprised, "The mind?!"

"Yes! We get caught up in the vicious cycle of the senses because of our mind. Our mind instigates us with all kinds of sensory pleasures. It starts demanding whatever it sees. This has been ailing humanity since ancient times. That's why our ancestors likened the human body to a chariot. The five horses attached to the chariot represent our senses. The mind is the charioteer. We are the travelers seated in this chariot moving towards our goal. If we sit quietly without deciding the goal of our life, the mind will take charge of the chariot and take it wherever it wants.

"When we see a nice restaurant, the tongue starts craving the taste of food. When we see a theatre, the eyes start craving the scenes of a movie. When the temperature is too high, the urge to have a cold drink will arise. When we see a mall or apparel showroom, the desire to adorn our body raises its head.

"In this way, many desires will arise in the journey of life, and our senses will thoughtlessly hanker after them. If we don't train our charioteer, i.e., the mind, and clearly define the goal of our life, the mind will loosen the reins of its sense-horses instead of tightening them. All the sense-horses will go helter-skelter in different directions leading the chariot into total disarray."

Devesh was intently listening to Grandpa. He suddenly remarked, "Okay! Now I got it. If the mind is aware of our goal, it can guide our chariot in the right direction. But how do we train the mind? The senses generate new desires every day. One desire today, another tomorrow! Does this mean we shouldn't have any desires?"

"No! I don't mean that. We are not talking about giving up or relinquishing anything. But when we become slaves to our desires, when we amass things that we don't need just because we see others having them, we should get the mind to understand the futility of acquiring those things. Once the mind understands the right direction, our chariot will persevere towards our goal. A wise charioteer always holds the reins firmly. Only a trained mind can help us achieve our goal.

"Mind is the sixth sense that nature has specially bestowed on human beings. Nature has bestowed all other beings with only five senses. Only humans have the mind that can discriminate between right and wrong. We can give the right direction to our life with the help of the mind. If the mind and senses work in tandem and are driven by discernment, it becomes easy to achieve our goal and success."

Devesh interrupted, "'But Grandpa, many people don't know about this and yet achieve their goals without training their minds."

Grandpa looked at the street from the balcony and asked, "Look at those people. Some are roaming around; some are standing by the side of the road and gossiping. What do you think their goal could be?"

"I don't know much about them. But some people may have a goal of earning good money, getting a promotion in their job, giving a quality life to their family, etc."

Grandpa asked, "Are these goals big or small?"

"These are small goals. Those who have big goals will be very busy at work."

Grandpa patted Devesh and exclaimed, "Well said! Small goals are achieved easily. But those, who have decided and achieved bigger goals, unknowingly learned to direct their mind and senses in the right direction."

"How can you say that?"

Grandpa smiled, "Okay! Name any successful person."

Devesh mused for a while and then asked, "From which field, Grandpa? Because there are so many names in different fields."

Grandpa said, "Take any field. Be it a businessman, a cricketer, someone in the film industry, or a technology innovator."

Devesh replied, "I know many such names, but some that come to my mind now are A.P.J. Abdul Kalam, Ratan Tata, Sundar Pichai, and Lata Mangeshkar."

Grandpa chirped happily, "That's good. Now tell me, how did they succeed? What if they were stuck in the diktat of their senses? Had they spent their time watching web series, looking for new avenues to enjoy food, back-biting or gossiping, would they have succeeded?"

Devesh was struck by surprise, "Superb! I never thought on these lines, Grandpa. None of these great people would have wasted their time indulging in their senses. What you said is right. Those who have set big goals do not get caught up in sensory pleasures."

Grandpa asked Devesh, "Yes! But would it have been easy for them? They would have also been tempted to copy others. The illusory attractions of the world would have tried to seduce them too. But they understood the value of their time. They stuck to their goal. The passion for doing something perfect did not allow them to get entangled in the desires of their senses.

"Most importantly, they trained their minds to safeguard themselves from all this to achieve success. For some people, this happens naturally. But some others have to train themselves consciously to achieve their goal."

Devesh assured Grandpa, "Yes, Grandpa! I got it. I need to train myself to achieve my goal."

Devesh's mobile rang. Devesh said, "Grandpa, that's enough for today. I need to visit my friend to work on a college project."

"That's fine. But do reflect on which of your senses give rise to what desires by tomorrow? You need to write down at least three desires for each of your senses. Is that okay?"

Devesh smiled, "Sure… Bye, Grandpa!"

To be continued on page 79

7

The Confluence of the Mind And the Senses

Just like words, put together, form a sentence, thoughts gather to form the mind. The mind holds the reins of the five senses but gets entangled in sensory desires too.

Our five senses constantly focus on the outside world. Our mind records whatever we see, hear, smell, touch, and taste. For example, all the scenes that our eyes see are recorded within us, creating a mental album. Due to these recorded impressions, new desires are incessantly born within us. When you see a new model of a car, the mind immediately prompts, "What a beautiful car! I wish I had a similar car!" Thus, the eyes behold countless scenes throughout the day, and with every scene, the mind keeps augmenting its desires.

This happens with every sense. Our mind records the smallest and the biggest of sensory perceptions and keeps forming desires. This happens knowingly or unknowingly. The desire arises to repeat what pleases the mind and the senses and avoid or escape what displeases them.

Thus, thoughts of the past and future arise in our mind based on whatever we have experienced through our five senses and how our mind has perceived it all. Our mind is just a bundle of thoughts.

Right from birth, nature has bestowed us with the power to think and feel emotions in response to sensory perceptions. When a thought or feeling gets associated with the senses, the world begins to take shape within the mind.

The mind has two facets—intuitive and spontaneous, judgmental and opinionated. The intuitive facet always encourages you to act naturally to the best of your abilities, while the judgmental facet keeps posing hurdles in this natural and intuitive flow. Thus, the mind can be divided into two faculties—the intuitive mind and the contrast mind.

The intuitive mind dwells in the present and functions based on one's qualities. When one functions with the intuitive mind, he gives his best. Thoughts arise in the intuitive mind spontaneously by inspiration and are acted upon naturally.

On the contrary, the contrast mind dwells in the past or the future. It weaves stories about situations, events, people, and anything at large. It compares and weighs incidents, people, or objects and says, "This is good; that is bad."

For example, a software engineer developed a new software solution. He wanted to present it to his organization before launching it in the market. As soon as his intuitive mind found a goal, all his senses started working in unison to come up with the presentation.

But when his contrast mind came into play, he started thinking, "God knows how the audience will receive my presentation! Despite working so hard, what if people don't like this solution? What if I only get a few orders? It will be a great loss; all my hard work will go in vain. What will be my future?" and so on.

As soon as such thoughts arose, his mind was overwhelmed with fear, anxiety, and apprehension. This hampered the quality of his work. In a hurry, he commited some mistakes in his presentation; he forgot to include some important points about the solution. All his senses that were cooperating with the intuitive mind stopped doing so when the contrast mind took over.

All tasks can be performed naturally in the best way by being in the present. The past is memory and future is mere imagination, based on which the contrast mind puts spokes in the wheel of the intuitive mind. It disrupts or throws up doubts in the work being done in the present. The contrast mind needs to be trained to keep quiet so that the intuitive mind can function to the fullest, guiding the senses in the right direction.

For example, you are getting down the stairs in a building spontaneously and gracefully. Suddenly, your contrast mind throws up a thought, "I'm getting down the stairs so well... I hope I don't miss a step and fall...." There is a possibility that you will indeed overstep or miss a step and trip down the stairs!

In the post-pandemic period, many people work from home. All project meetings are conducted online. Imagine that you are participating in such a meeting. Everything is happening intuitively. Suddenly, your contrast mind flags red, "Listen to your volume! Everyone at home is watching you and wondering what's up; why are you talking so loudly?" As soon as this thought arises, you feel awkward and forget what you wanted to share and discuss in the meeting."

Let us understand this with one more example. Rakesh was looking out of his window. While some people were passing by the road, some children were shouting at each other while playing. Suddenly, his attention zeroed in on a crimson-colored sporty-looking car coming that way. He liked the car's contours and funky color so much that soon he got preoccupied with the thoughts of the car. A desire arose in his mind, "If only I had such a car, we would have driven out in it; it would have been fun going places with friends. But now, I cannot afford this car." Rakesh, unknowingly, was lost in these thoughts for a long time. Suddenly, he was startled to hear his friend's voice, who was standing behind and calling him for a while. Rakesh was so engrossed in his thoughts that he could not hear anything. What happened to Rakesh often happens to us too.

When Rakesh's senses were attentively focused outside, his intuitive mind was at work, but his contrast mind sprang into action as soon as his eyes fell on the car. The sight which gave him joy started making him sad as his mind began diving into the future and considering his limitations. This is how the contrast mind functions. It makes you wallow in sorrow, lures you in every possible way, and then gets you to fulfill the desire.

The mind is full of desires like seeking credit, gaining social recognition, enjoying luxuries, etc. It rejoices in idle fantasies, tries to safeguard its egoic identity, and even enjoys at the cost of others. By flattery, it becomes a slave to the habit of craving and gratification of the senses in the false hope of satisfaction. Introspect on your life and notice the endless list of desires that keep arising within you in a day.

Day by day, the bag of desires keeps growing, and man spends his entire life fulfilling them. The sad part is that people have made the gratification of sensory desires the goal of their life. Hence, those who intend to achieve the true goal of life must safeguard themselves from gratifying their senses and train their mind for it.

The good news is that the mind, which is the master of our senses, is our servant. We will learn about its training in detail in the next chapter.

8

Celibate the Senses

Countless desires arise in our mind every day, though we may not be aware of them. The desires that we energize with our attention manifest in our life. Otherwise, desires merely remain passing thoughts.

The question is, which desires should we energize? And the simple answer is that we should energize those desires that help us achieve the goal of our life. This exercise comprises of three steps. Let us understand them in detail.

First step: Understand the tendencies of your senses

It is not wrong to have desires. But when one gratifies the cravings of his senses every time, it becomes a tendency. Later, this tendency becomes a hindrance in achieving his goal. Hence, it is necessary to eradicate this tendency.

For example, a person is fond of relishing sweets. On seeing sweets, he can't hold himself back from binging on them. Slowly, it becomes a tendency as he cannot live without having sweets.

Similarly, some people are habituated to listening to music while working or studying. This helps their mind to work efficiently. If music is not available, they say, "I can't work without music," or "I can't study without music." Thus, they stop working because of this habit of the mind.

To break this tendency, make all your senses celibate. Yes! You are not being asked to be celibate but rather to make your senses celibate so that none of your senses will provoke you to make choices that do not align with your goal.

Making the senses celibate does not mean that you won't have delicious food or listen to music. You will do what you like, but you won't create a tendency that you can't live without. Otherwise, one or the other sense weakens your resolve, due to which you keep vacillating over your choices.

For example, a student wants to study. But when he sees his favorite TV program, he completely forgets about his studies and gets engrossed in watching the program. Here, he has changed his choice. Instead of studying, he chooses to gratify the desires of his senses. Therefore, make the senses celibate so that **you see, listen, or do only what you have decided**.

Second Step: Learn to make new choices

The untrained mind can never make the right choice. It often gets bogged down with choices, like, "Should I do this or that? Should I go here or there?" It is easy to choose between two options. But when one needs to choose between 4 to 5 options, one gets perplexed. If you come across such a situation, you will face a similar dilemma. Hence, you need to train your mind in advance to remind it of your life goal to make the right choice that aligns with your goal.

Consider that your friends are planning to watch a movie. Then, they intend to shop and dine at a mall. You also want to accompany them, but you need to prepare for your exams scheduled after a week. In this case, what would you do? Would you follow the diktat of your senses and join your friends, or focus on your bright future? You alone can make this choice; no one else can choose on your behalf. When you choose in favor of your goal, your mind also understands that you want to achieve higher possibilities in life and supports you completely. Thus, as your decisions begin to align with your goal even a couple of times, you will experience that your mental resolve grows stronger.

You would have heard the story of the well-known Indian classical dancer, Sudha Chandran. She lost one of her legs in a road accident when she was sixteen. Doctors discovered that her right leg was developing gangrene and proposed amputation. She was operated upon and fixed with a prosthetic leg, which helped her gain some mobility. However, not the one to lose courage, Sudha Chandran firmly resolved to train her legs to dance again. She worked hard tirelessly till she was able to perform brilliantly. She earned worldwide recognition with her spellbinding dance performances. She gained success owing to the right choice and firm resolve to abide by it.

In the same way, whatever you are experiencing in your life today is the result of your past choices. So, check –

- What have been your choices so far - waking up sluggishly at 8 a.m. or getting up and practicing yoga or exercises at 5 a.m.?
- Which field have you chosen for your studies or profession, and why?
- Whom did you choose as your friends?
- What kind of food have you usually chosen for your meals?

Who can make such choices for you? You alone can! It's entirely up to you. Initially, you may find it difficult to make this choice, but with time, making choices that align with your goal will become second nature to you.

Third step: Look out for options to choose

Quite often, our mind and senses get caught up in external attractions because we lose sight of any other choice available to us at that time. So, we allow the mind and senses to be engrossed in these attractions. At such times, exercise the third step of exploring at least ten other options to safeguard yourself from the temptations of your mind.

For example, your mind wants to play a game on the mobile because you see no other obvious option. Remind yourself of your goal and note down at least ten options at such times. Instead of gaming on the mobile, you can read a good book, pursue some creative work, watch an informative program on TV, listen to some motivational talk, help someone with their work, discuss some constructive topic with your friend, etc.

Likewise, keep a list of options ready for all those situations where you tend to indulge your mind and senses and go astray. You will move towards your goal instead of getting caught up in sensory pleasures when you have thought over options that align with your goal. Thus, practicing these three steps will yield desirable results in your life.

Karat karat abhyaas ke jadmati hot sujaan,

Rasari aawat jaat ke sil par parat nishaan.

The above couplet was composed by Vrind - the renowned Hindi poet. Even seemingly unachievable tasks can be accomplished with relentless hard work. The sword of persistent practice can not only rip through the tendencies of the mind but also eliminate inertia. Consistent practice is the hallmark of success.

9

Develop Your Focus First, Then Attain Your Goal

You can fly a kite high up in the sky as much as you want, provided it is tied to a string that you wield. An unstrung kite is like a dry leaf swirling in the breeze. It does not have any resolute existence of its own and keeps wading aimlessly in the sky. It cannot fly by itself unless you properly tie it to a string and guide it according to the direction of the wind.

Here, the kite represents our goal. The string represents our mind and senses that should be tied to our goal. The direction of the wind is the focus of the mind.

You would have noticed that sometimes the kite gets buoyed up by itself with the gust of wind; you don't have to work it upward. But when the wind does not blow, you have to work hard at tugging the string to give the kite the necessary lift, and you become exhausted by the end of the day.

Similarly, success is inevitable when you bind the string of your mind and senses to your goal and give it a lift with the wind of your mental focus. However, when people are unclear about their goal, they cannot guide their mind and senses in the right direction. If your mind does not know what to do and where to go, it will become your master and lead you to wander aimlessly and indulge in sensory pleasures. Hence, it is essential to stay focused to work towards your goal without faltering. If the mind is not focused, its quality deteriorates even in performing trivial tasks.

For example, a housewife is cooking. Suddenly, she remembers a past incident and gets engrossed in those thoughts. As a result, she forgets to add some ingredients to the food preparation. Although she is proficient in cooking and everyone appreciates her culinary skills, her cooking is rendered tasteless as soon as she loses focus.

A student aims to study hard and top his exams. But whenever he searches for something related to his studies on Google, his eyes get distracted and caught up in topics unrelated to his goal, and he loses his focus.

This happens with everyone. When you sit to meditate or worship, your mind wanders in various topics, either hearing a noise in the kitchen or some mental scene. Although you may go through the physical ritual of worship, the purpose of worship, which is to feel pure and blissful, is not achieved. On the contrary, you may feel irritated as you seem to go through the motions without keeping a genuine intent.

Some people go to the market to buy some essential items, but an intense urge to eat something tangy or spicy arises within them, and they leave everything else to gratify this desire first. Later, they forget to buy some of the essential items or end up buying unnecessary things.

These are some trivial examples from our daily life. But if we want to achieve a big goal in our life and our mind cannot focus and gets entangled in the senses, it becomes increasingly challenging to achieve that goal. To prevent this, we must train our mind and senses to be focused. Enhance the quality of focus so that the mind supports us in progressing towards the goal without any hindrance.

A focused mind is like a searchlight that can help to easily find the tiniest of things, far-flung in the dark. It helps to deeply introspect every aspect of our life and weed out the smallest of shortcomings.

It is seen that goldsmiths, blacksmiths, carpenters, and weavers have a strong power of focus. They acquire this power through practice, not by reading books or listening to lectures. With consistent practice, we can also develop this quality of focus.

1. **Set a timer and focus** – Consider that you have resolved to study for some time, but the thought of listening to music or watching a movie on your mobile disturbs you. At such times, you can delay this desire for sense gratification by fixing some time for your mind to focus. Tell your mind, "I will study for an hour, and only then use the mobile phone," or "I will use the mobile phone only for 15 minutes and then study." Set the timer on any of your gadgets to complete your study with full focus.

2. **Dedicate yourself to the goal** – After setting your goal, deeply connect with it so that you will be reminded of it day and night, in and through all activities. When Sachin Tendulkar was asked the secret of his success, he said, "I keep thinking of cricket only for 24 hours a day. There have been very few days when I have not been to the ground for net practice."

   We should also cultivate the same dedication, intense passion, and unshakable perseverance toward our goal. Let us understand this with a mythological story.

   Lord Indra was angry with the farmers in a village and had cursed them, "There will be no rain in the village for twelve years; your fields will remain barren." The farmers had no choice but to wait. All the farmers gave up working in the fields and stayed back in their homes. They thought, "What is the point in sowing the seeds when it's not going to rain!"

A farmer named Kishan lived in that village with his two sons. He heard about all this. Yet, he went to his field with his sons and started tilling and sowing seeds. The other farmers mocked him, "Don't you know that it won't rain in this village for the next twelve years? What's the use of farming?" Kishan calmly replied, "Yes, I've heard that it won't rain," and continued working, teaching his sons. Three to four years passed this way. Lord Indra was alarmed seeing him, "What is he doing after all? If there's no water, how will the crops grow? Why is he working in vain?" Disguised as a Brahmin, Lord Indra approached him and asked, "Have you not heard of the curse? Why are you still working so hard?"

Kishan replied, "Yes, I've heard about the curse. Yet, I'm doing my duty, just as Lord Indra does his. If I stay at home for twelve years, I will forget farming, and if I forget, what will I teach my sons? Hence, I am working now to have no difficulty in farming when it starts raining after twelve years."

Seeing Kishan's dedication, Lord Indra began showering rain. Kishan had already sown the seeds, so he had bumper produce that year. The other farmers were idling away, and their land remained barren. They did not reap any benefit even when it rained.

Likewise, when one works relentlessly towards his goal with dedication, just like Lord Indra, one's senses also have a change of heart and get ready to support him.

3. ***Traatak* meditation*** - You can enhance your power of focus by practicing the Traatak meditation. Focus on some object like a candle flame without blinking your eyes and remain seated in that posture for a long time. This makes your mind more

---

* To understand 'Traatak meditation' in detail, read the book titled "The Magic of Willpower," authored by Sirshree

alert and raises your ability to remain aware and vigilant for prolonged periods.

Whatever work you do consistently with awareness is a practice of concentration. When you are focused, there are no thoughts. When there are thoughts, you are not focused. Concentration is single-pointed awareness devoid of thoughts. Work done consciously with such razor-sharp focus leads you to your goal quickly. On the contrary, work done unconsciously with a distracted mind gets delayed and deteriorates. Let us focus our mind and senses on achieving our goal and making our life beautiful.

10

Intellect Over Mind

Prince Indra used to top in all the competitions at the hermitage. Everyone loved and admired him. He also respected everyone. Once, when he topped a very challenging competition, his guru was so impressed by his proficiency that he offered him a ride on a flying elephant.

Prince Indra happily mounted the elephant along with the mahout and set out on an excursion to roam around the town. The mahout held a unique goad to control and guide the elephant's movements. While passing over a garden, they stopped for some time. When they were resting in the garden, a sage saw them. He was impressed with the prince's aura and envisioned that the prince would grow up to be a majestic king. He felt like offering a garland of flowers to the prince. He collected some flowers, made a beautiful garland, and invited the prince to wear it. The prince got down from the elephant and walked towards the sage. He bowed down with humility and touched the revered feet. Pleased with his behavior, the sage offered him the garland and blessed him, "May you attain the echelons of heaven!" The prince returned happily.

The blessing greatly influenced the prince's life. With every year, he kept progressing further. As he grew up, his contrast mind also developed alongside the intuitive mind. His ego began to raise its head. A few years later, he again topped the competition at the hermitage and again got the opportunity to ride the flying elephant.

During his pleasure flight, he passed over yet another beautiful garden. He was fascinated by the enchanting vistas of the garden and expressed his desire to get down there. He decided to stay overnight and asked the mahout to come back the next morning to pick him up. On hearing this, the mahout left with his goad.

To his surprise, he met the same sage who was pleased to see him again. Yet again, the sage offered him a garland of marigold flowers. But now, since he had grown up and was soon to be crowned, his egoic mind had lost its value for the sage's benevolence. As soon as the sage placed the garland around his neck, he took it off and hurled it toward the elephant. Being an animal with lower consciousness, the elephant tossed the garland onto its back. As the mahout was not around to restrain the elephant, the garland fell, and soon, the elephant crushed it under its feet. This infuriated the sage. He cursed the prince, "Your ship will sink," and walked away.

Let us understand the pointers in this analogy. Prince Indra symbolizes the senses. As a child, he was ready to receive everything intuitively.

When a child is small, he is close to his heart. He functions with his intuitive mind. At that time, he accepts whatever he receives with love and respect. It could be praise, knowledge, or guidance by an accomplished soul. But as he grows up, the ego and the contrast mind begin to develop within him. He starts judging people and incidents as superior or inferior, civilized or barbaric, rich or poor, sinful or virtuous, respectable or disrespectable, good or bad, etc.

The elephant symbolizes the contrast mind, which goes astray in the absence of the mahout. When the mind is uncontrolled, one indulges in various sensory desires and lands himself in troublesome situations. Many movies depict people playing pranks like kidnapping someone, demanding ransom, or even committing murders. Their entire life is ruined with such indiscriminate indulgences.

One needs to reflect on one's life and assess which sensory indulgences he is immersed in, whether he is digging his own grave with them. Everything should be done in the right measure. The mahout's presence is necessary to exercise this control.

The mahout and his goad symbolize the discerning power of the human intellect. If one receives the highest knowledge but doesn't have the discerning power to apply it, he will most likely ignore the knowledge or misuse it for his selfish gains. Thus, the same knowledge that could have elevated him to new heights pushes him into the abyss of darkness, becoming a curse for him. In this case, when the prince asked the mahout to leave him alone and return the next day with the goad, the blessing bestowed on him turned into a curse.

Similarly, when the contrast mind drives one's life, one trusts the mind and senses and gets deluded. When Prince Indra asks the mahout to leave him and return the next day, it symbolizes the decision to abandon one's power of discerning the truth. As "tomorrow" never comes, one continues to indulge in the mind and senses without paying heed to one's conscience.

We should use the goad of discerning power to restrain our mind and senses. The mahout symbolizes the power of discernment. Always keep the mahout with you. Never ask him to leave you and return tomorrow. Instead, hold onto wisdom, and ask the greed and desires of your mind and senses to leave you and come "tomorrow."

If you are clear about whom you will ask to leave and come tomorrow and whom you will ask to always stay with you, you can easily restrain your mind with the goad of discernment.

For example, when your ears yearn to hear some bickering or gossip, tell them, "Hey, listen to it tomorrow." When the tongue wants to abuse someone, tell the tongue, "O tongue, you can abuse tomorrow." When a sinful thought arises, tell it, "O sin, come tomorrow." Tell the frightening nightmares, "O nightmare, come tomorrow."

The sensory indulgences are like chewing gum. Initially, it tastes sweet and delicious. As you keep chewing it, you indulge in its sweetness. Once you are tired of chewing it, your entire focus is on where to throw it and how soon you can get rid of it. Similarly, the senses are appeased until they are immersed in worldly pleasures. They constantly hanker after the avenues for enjoyment. Although the conscience of the intuitive mind repeatedly warns, "Throw it, get rid of it," the contrast mind doesn't want to listen. At such times, become alert and aware, wield your discerning power, and guide your senses in the right direction.

11

Purifying the Mind and Senses

Who doesn't like a clean environment! But what if someone appears clean and benevolent on the outside but is internally deceitful and stuck in selfishly gratifying his sensory desires? People will be associated with such a person only for a brief period. They will keep away as soon as they know the person's hidden nature.

The question is how the mind and senses get contaminated, how their cleansing is going to help, and how to cleanse them. Let us understand this with an analogy.

There was a village led by a village headman named Suryamukhi. Every day, he would wear a special shirt and go to the village council's meeting place to attend the council and resolve public issues. His shirt had five outer pockets and one inner pocket. He would keep some documents pertaining to law and order in each of these pockets. He would listen to each problem, take out a document from a pocket, and suggest a solution as per the law specified in that document. He knew which pocket contained the specific document that mentioned the rules to solve a particular problem. He would precisely fetch the right document from that pocket, read it, and resolve the issue. After solving and deciding upon some of these matters, he would return home, have dinner, and go to bed. Every morning, he would wash his shirt with soap, rinse and put it for drying in the sun.

Let us now understand the pointers in this analogy.

- The village represents life on Earth.
- The village headman's shirt symbolizes the human body.
- The five outer pockets are our five senses.
- The single inner pocket represents our mind.
- The law and order documents symbolize the knowledge of Truth, the knowledge of life on Earth.
- The soap stands for the practice of meditation and conscious chanting of a mantra.
- Washing and rinsing represent the purification of the mind and senses and guiding them in the right direction.
- The sunlight is Consciousness (or Self, Allah, God).

We have come on Earth with our body, its five senses, the mind, and the intellect. We move around with them throughout the day and carry out our worldly activities. We use our mind and senses to overcome any challenges we may face in financial, social, physical, or mental aspects of life. But over a period, a lot of mental filth gathers on our mind and senses, due to which we find it difficult to overcome life's challenges.

What is this filth? It is nothing but the invisible layers of wrong or limiting beliefs and impure thoughts that have been accumulating in our mind for years together. These invisible layers skew the lens of perception through which we experience the world. The mind is ever engrossed in gratifying sensory desires in anticipation of feeling complete, but desires are insatiable. Just like a serpent raises its hood, the mind raises its head as soon as the can of endless desires is opened.

Whenever we encounter any incident, the contrast mind immediately begins to weigh, compare, and make assumptions about the incident. It affixes a label of good or bad to it. It becomes either happy or sad after drawing conclusions. The challenge becomes a "problem" because of the dirt of the contrast mind and senses, and we unknowingly try to solve it with the same contrast mind. How can the one that has created the problem be the solution to it? It is like asking a thief to safeguard our house! The contrast mind can never provide the right solution and happiness. Hence, purifying our mind is as important as purifying our body.

Consider how you would feel if you were to visit someplace wearing soiled clothes? The thought of being dirty will constantly bug you and make you feel uncomfortable. On the other hand, when you wear clean and pressed attire, it boosts your confidence. Similarly, when our mind is pure and our senses are wisely guided in the right direction, we can overcome all challenges easily because we perceive the problem from a pure and neutral perspective.

This is possible only when we consistently practice meditation and cleanse our mind and senses with the shower of divine grace. In other words, by sitting in meditation, we bring our mind, body, and senses into alignment with pure consciousness.

Having aligned yourself with the divine flow in meditation, when you return to the world, you watch the world with an awakened eye. You cast away the past – whatever happened yesterday, what someone said, what stories were woven by the biased mind. You start witnessing the world as it is without affixing any labels. Just as clothes become bright and shining after a good wash, you start looking at every incident with a positive outlook after cleansing the mind in meditation.

At times, the villagers were not pleased with the village headman's decisions because he attended the meeting wearing an unwashed shirt that day. The day he would wear a washed shirt, his decisions would prove right and bring joy to all.

In much the same way, as you meditate consistently, your mind gradually becomes pure and virtuous; you feel blissful within;

wisdom awakens within you, and all your problems are not only solved but dissolve!

The greater the quality of the soap of meditation, the finer is the quality of inner cleansing. This is possible when you clean each pocket of your shirt inside-out and dry it in the sun. This means that the quality of meditation and life improves when you keenly witness the subtler aspects of life during meditation. You become aware of the slightest negative feelings with an attitude of detachment and dwell in the experience of untouched beingness.

Let us practice the following meditation to enhance the quality of life. First, read the instructions completely and then sit in a comfortable posture before closing your eyes.

1. During meditation, thoughts of sensory pleasures or ambitions may arise. Remind yourself that you will set aside a separate timeslot to think about them. Invest this precious time of meditation to dwell only in the experience of your beingness. If this time is spent properly, all decisions made after meditation will be perfect. They will arise from the right reference point.

2. Witness all the aspects of life and notice your perspective towards different situations - where do the impurities of the mind like wrong beliefs, comparisons, and labels overwhelm you? Witness all of this.

3. Having witnessed all the negative aspects in the light of awareness, release them. For this, repeatedly affirm to yourself three to four times, "I am releasing all the negative thoughts and feelings from within me... Let go... Let go... Let go..."

4. Now, move on to the subtler aspects. Even if the slightest thorn pricks, i.e., even the minutest negative feeling is felt within, dissolve it. For example, you felt hurt when someone mocked you jokingly. Regard this as a thorn, a subtle feeling. Release it by telling your mind, "I am releasing all

the subtler negative thoughts and feelings... Let go... Let go... Let go..."

5. After this subtle cleansing, the flame of wisdom is kindled within you. You begin to perceive situations from a refined and untainted point of view. With the help of this eye of wisdom, witness how the so-called "problems" that you perceived earlier are not "problems" per se. In other words, witness all your problems dissolve. Just as the village head used to solve the villagers' problems by taking out different documents of law and order from his pockets, you also need to witness your problems being dissolved in the light of meditation and wisdom.

6. Now, slowly open your eyes.

The solution to every problem already exists. But since we are not aware, we get entangled in the problems and lament over them. We have never tried to know our true nature - our sense of beingness. We have never coached our senses to calm down or trained our mind to sit in one place for a while. Due to the impurities that sully the clarity of the mind, we are unable to tap into the solutions that are already available within us. Now, you can practice the above meditation technique to purify your mind and senses whenever you want.

12

The Futility of Satiating The Mind and Senses

You would have heard the Indian spiritual doctrine, "There is no end to desires. When one becomes free of desires, one is liberated from the cycle of birth and death forever." We all know that desires are the root cause of bondage in life, yet most of us are unable to break free of this web of desires. Isn't this surprising? What could be the reason? Why do we remain entangled in desires for our entire life? A person who is on his deathbed too holds on to some desire!

The story of King Yayati of Hastinapur demonstrates this enigma of human life. Yayati was the second son of King Nahush of the Chandravanshi dynasty. As King Nahush's elder son Yati had renounced the throne and became an ascetic, Yayati was coronated.

Yayati married Devayani, the daughter of Sage Shukracharya. Devayani's friend, Sharmishtha, accompanied her as her maid to Yayati's palace. Yayati had promised Sage Shukracharya that he would not court any woman other than Devayani. But despite giving his word, he fell for Sharmishtha and courted her.

Devayani got to know about this only after Sharmishtha gave birth to Yayati's son. She immediately complained about this to her father, Shukracharya. Infuriated at his son-in-law's infidelity, Shukracharya cursed Yayati that he would suffer untimely old age and impotence right away.

Yayati begged for forgiveness. Finally, Sage Shukracharya changed his mind and offered a solution, "If you can persuade any youngster to offer their youth to you in exchange for your old age, you can escape the curse and regain your lost youth."

Yayati wanted to continue to enjoy and satiate his sensual desires but had grown old and impotent because of the curse. He asked his five sons whether any of them would give up their youth to rejuvenate him. None of them were prepared for this, except his youngest son, Puru. He was just in his teens.

Man loses his discerning power when he lusts for sensual pleasures. Yayati was prepared to selfishly snatch his teenage son's youth to satisfy his own endless lust despite having grown old. He was thrilled to get back his youth at the cost of his son's youth. Regaining his youth was like adding oil to the self-perpetuating fire of lust.

But Puru's selfless and giving attitude touched Yayati. Perplexed, he asked Puru, "My dear son, how did you become prepared to sacrifice your youth?" Puru answered, "O father, you have spent your entire life trying to satiate your sensory cravings. I could see that you are still discontented! Observing your life, I have understood that hankering after sensory pleasures is futile. It can never lead to true happiness."

Thereafter, Yayati enjoyed sensual pleasure for a thousand years. After experiencing the fire of lust to the fullest, he finally realized its futility and understood that the pleasures he chased throughout his life were just a mirage. It was an illusion of happiness!

He crowned Puru as the king and retired into a secluded life of severe penance. After incurring the merit of intense penance, Yayati ascended to heaven. But soon, Lord Indra cursed him for his arrogance and cast him off to the lower levels on Earth. He met his grandsons, Ashta and Shivi, and some sages on his celestial way back to Earth. Seeing Yayati's grief at being banished to the netherworld, they offered the merit of their penance to help him return to heaven. Finally, Yayati attained liberation with their help.

This story has two main characters. One is King Yayati, who realized the illusory nature of sensory pleasures only after indulging in them for thousand years. The other is Puru, who contemplated his father's life at a very early age and realized that mere gratification of desires could never yield lasting contentment.

The final words of King Yayati were, "**It is not that I indulged in the pleasures; rather, the pleasures indulged me.** I didn't consume sensory enjoyments; instead, I got consumed by them!" Indeed! When we blindly chase desires, we don't devour them; they devour us. When we fail to eradicate our desires, the desires eliminate us. Time never perishes, but we perish with time.

Man hankers after desires for his entire life, and finally, desires enslave him. He becomes so attached to desires that he loses his ability to discriminate between freedom and bondage. He never realizes that he is not devouring the senses; the senses are devouring him.

Man wanders about in the illusory world with his mind and senses, where everything allures him. He feels, "I should have everything that I like." When he fails to achieve something, he feels angry and irritated. If the desire to have something remains unfulfilled, he feels distressed. And if the desire is satiated, he becomes arrogant and starts longing for something new. This vicious cycle of desires keeps going on and on. Until one does not introspect on his life, greed and sorrow keep haunting him.

When one listens to a story of Yayati and Puru, or goes through some adverse incident, one is driven to contemplate the futility of sensory pursuits and the truth of life. Nature presents an interval for contemplation between two incidents so that one can reflect on various aspects of life to attain the ultimate goal of life. When one honestly undertakes deep introspection on his life, he learns to live life in a true sense. These contemplation opportunities help one rectify one's mistakes and progress further. But, if one laments over the situation instead of contemplating it, he loses interest in life.

Hence, follow the principle, "Think a little, but right here and right now." Invest at least five to ten minutes every day to develop the habit of contemplation. This can lend the right direction to your life. Without contemplation, life goes in vain. Those who contemplate work on themselves and gradually progress towards true freedom in life.

It is often observed that unwritten contemplation proves futile later because we tend to forget many finer aspects with time. Hence, always use writing material like a diary, a pen, or a laptop for contemplation. Written contemplation leads us towards a brighter future. So, let's grab this opportunity for contemplation.

Whenever a desire arises in your mind, for example, to watch a movie or buy the latest mobile, ask yourself: Even if I did fulfill this desire, how long will the pleasure last? Is this pleasure permanent? How long will I keep pleasing my senses?

In this manner, whenever a new desire arises, and you ask yourself these questions with awareness, you will see through the temporary nature of these sensory pleasures. Such repeated questioning will weaken the power of the desires. Then you will shift your quest from momentary pleasures to eternal bliss.

In the next section, we will explore how to experience permanent bliss.

PART 3
Turning the Senses Inward

...Concluding

Devesh was busy with his college project for the next three days. On the fourth day, his Grandpa was preparing to return to his village when Devesh met him.

Devesh asked him, "What happened, Grandpa? Where are you going? You were to stay longer."

"Yes, my son! I need to return to our village. I have been called. But what brings you home so early today? It is just noon now!"

"Grandpa, I was busy with my group project for the past three days. This morning we submitted the project, and I immediately rushed home to be with you. How are you traveling?"

"Your dad is sending the car and driver to drop me off."

"Okay… I'll accompany you if you're going by car," said Devesh happily.

Grandpa cautioned him, "But you need to attend your lectures at the college. It takes seven to eight hours to reach the village, and the car will return only tomorrow."

"No problem, Grandpa! I have a holiday tomorrow. We have been continuously working on the group project for the last three days. So, we have been allowed to take the day off tomorrow. I will take this opportunity to visit our village along with you. It has been a long time since I last visited. It will be a break for me too. I will feel rejuvenated in the open natural atmosphere of the village."

"Then it's fine. Since you're coming along, we can also discuss on the way. Take your essentials with you."

"Yes, Grandpa. I'll make a couple of phone calls. We'll have lunch and then leave."

After an hour, they left for the village.

Grandpa asked Devesh, "How much could you work on training your mind?"

Devesh replied, "Frankly speaking, my mind and senses were completely absorbed in the project. I didn't feel like doing anything else."

Grandpa cautioned him, "Those who have higher goals guide their mind and senses in the right direction and safeguard themselves from being trapped in Maya."

"But Grandpa, at times, don't we control our sensory desires as per our priorities? Why does everyone need to master their senses? Does everyone need to have higher goals? Is it wrong for people like us who are leading a simple life to gratify their desires?"

Grandpa smiled, "I knew these questions would arise. It is not about being right or wrong. It is about what you want to achieve in your life. If you are content with the smaller mundane goals in life, you will seldom posit higher goals. You will not want to train your senses accordingly. But, if you want to do something big, something new, something different, something extraordinary in your life that will take your life to an entirely new level, you will have to guide your senses in the right direction; you will have to train them for the higher goal. Only then will you feel contented in life."

"Grandpa, is there any other goal besides attaining fame, a respectable social position, or financial status in life?"

"All these merely help to sustain our livelihood. The actual purpose of human birth is beyond all of this."

Devesh asked in awe, "Is that so? And what is that Grandpa?"

"We are gifted the senses to make our life simple and smooth so that, with the help of our senses, we can attain Mission Earth – the sole purpose of life. But the converse has happened. All beings on Earth have got the same kind of senses. Of these, birds and animals use their senses intuitively and live a balanced life. But we humans are also gifted with a conscious choice of how to use our senses. Neglecting this faculty of higher choice, we have got entangled and enslaved by our senses. Today, deluded by allurements, we have assumed gratification of the senses as our goal instead of using them for the higher purpose."

"Those who gained control over their senses, guided them in the right direction, enhanced their capabilities, prioritized Mission Earth, and are remembered as the great masters who led truly successful lives."

"Grandpa, I understood everything else, but what is Mission Earth?"

"Our Mission Earth is to discover who we truly are, gain its understanding by experientially knowing it, and develop conviction of this understanding."

"'Who am I?' Oh, Grandpa! What's the big deal about this? I am Devesh; you are my Grandpa!"

Grandpa laughed, "Devesh, who you truly are is not the same as your body and mind, your name and form. You are beyond all of this. The journey of life is about discovering this."

"Grandpa, now you are confusing me!"

"You are neither the body nor the mind. You are their master! Mission Earth is about knowing your real Self as Pure Consciousness and expressing its qualities."

"Grandpa, we all refer to ourselves as our bodies and personalities. What is the real Self? What are its qualities? And how can I know them?"

"It is difficult to understand this topic intellectually because the true Self can be known only by directly experiencing it. Still, I will try to explain this in a simple way."

"Yes, thanks for trying, Grandpa! I'll try to understand it."

Grandpa explained, "To understand this, you first need to know that the senses are more powerful than the body, the mind is more powerful than the senses, the intellect is more powerful than the mind, and the Self is the most powerful. Our goal is to reach the Self.

"When the mind and intellect are inclined more towards the senses or the body, they choose to indulge in the illusory world of Maya. But when they gain the understanding of the Self and its real purpose, their choices begin to align with Mission Earth.

"To attain this state, you should train your senses so that when they confront the illusory world, they can be guided inward instead of getting caught up in sensory content. You may have seen the Touch-me-not plant that turns its leaves inward when touched. Likewise, the moment your senses get the touch of Maya, they should turn inward and become indifferent to the external stimuli. When you choose to follow such a practice of sensory prohibition, you move towards attaining the sole purpose of life - Mission Earth.

"On attaining the goal, the expression of the qualities of the Self is more pronounced. There are many qualities of the Self like unconditional love, unshakable peace, boundless joy, compassion, forgiveness, patience, courage, creativity, consistency, infallible faith, etc. But the prominent qualities are expressed as serving people with love, spreading peace, developing an eye of oneness, witnessing the One Consciousness or Self in all beings, dwelling in bliss, and so on. Thereafter, there is no more seeking happiness because one is forever established in supreme bliss."

...Concluding

"Oh my God! Grandpa, these things are so complicated to understand. I'm just a college-going student! Do I need to think about all this so early? Can't I understand them after I grow up and settle down?"

When Grandpa said nothing, Devesh wondered whether he had said something wrong. He, too, remained quiet. After some time, Grandpa asked the driver to stop the car and park it by the side of the road. There was a tea stall on the opposite side. Both Grandpa and the driver got down. Grandpa also signaled Devesh to follow.

They settled at a table outside the stall, and the driver went inside. There was a big ground in front, where some youngsters were busy with the net practice for cricket, football, and volleyball. There were arrangements for many other games too.

Grandpa broke the silence and said, "Devesh, life is also a game. You can live it either like a football or a volleyball."

Devesh was perplexed, "How is that so?"

"Have your tea first. Then we will go for a walk around the ground."

After having tea, they reached the ground.

"You are questioning the need for understanding these spiritual things now. You feel you can understand them after you grow up. But, if you want to lead a simple and smooth life like the volleyball, the sooner you understand it, the better."

"Grandpa, I did not get it."

Looking at the football practice, Grandpa asked Devesh, "Have you ever played football?"

Devesh replied, "No, I like to play volleyball."

Grandpa explained, "See, both the games are being practiced here. You would be aware that, whether in football or volleyball, the aim is to hit the ball such that you score points.

"In the case of football, the ball is kicked a lot to lead it into the goal. It keeps moving all over the place. However, in the case of volleyball, the ball is in the players' hands. The players shoot it without letting it fall.

"That's it! Our life is no different from a game. When we are not aware of our true Self, our life is like a football. Many problems and stress keep occurring in our lives owing to our desires. Our peace and happiness get kicked around all over the place. Finally, we overcome these difficulties and reach the goal, but we stumble across a lot in life until then.

"On the contrary, if we become aware of our true Self and train our senses and mind to turn within, our life will become like a volleyball. This means there would be fewer problems, and we would reach the goal easily, enjoying the path all the way without falling apart."

Devesh caught the insight, "Oh! Now I understand. If I truly know 'Who am I,' then my mind and senses would get less entangled in the outside world, and I would be able to live a simpler life. Now I understand why you are so resolved and disciplined in your life! You have imparted the same training to mom and dad, right?"

Grandpa concluded, "Yes, my son! This is the essence of life. And the earlier you grasp it, the better. There are no limitations on age to understand and practice this. On the contrary, if you start working on it right now, then with practice, you will get habituated to walking on this path by the time you grow up.

"People keep postponing the pursuit of higher understanding till old age, and when they grow old, they find it difficult to change themselves within as their tendencies have become deeply rooted by then. They waste their entire lives entangled in the senses and do not attain this understanding till death.

"If we attain Mission Earth and realize our true Self, our mind and senses remain in our control, and life will brim with ease, simplicity, and bliss!"

13

The Real Goal of The Mind and Senses

Once a person went to buy a bar of soap. The shopkeeper told him about the ongoing scheme of getting a free designer comb on buying two bars of soap. He got lured by this offer and bought two bars of soap.

After reaching home, instead of having a bath, he got engrossed in examining the comb. In addition to a beautiful design, the comb had many attractive features. As he combed his hair, music started playing from the comb, his hair started shining, and his scalp felt cool and fresh. He got deeply engrossed in these novel experiences and forgot about the soap completely.

This is exactly what is happening with us today. We have received this life on the Earth to experience the Self. We have also got the mind and senses for free to help us in this endeavor. But just like the comb in the above example, we have become so busy gratifying our mind and senses that we have forgotten our true purpose of being on Earth; rather, we are made to forget it. We strive hard to satiate the desires of our mind and senses, considering it the goal of life.

The basic purpose of life on Earth is to know the experience of Self and express its divine qualities. But it is lost somewhere in the charms of Maya and got buried under the layers of sensory experiences accumulated over time.

The pull of Maya is not just limited to sensory objects. The mind and senses can also get entangled in various incidents. Having seen something worth cherishing, the mind may get repeatedly drawn to it. It may yearn to visit a place. It may not be able to hold itself back from relishing certain tastes. It may crave a soothing touch again and again. It may become fascinated by a fragrance and wish to be immersed in that environment as long as possible. In turn, we get deluded by the attractions of Maya at the cost of forgetting our true Self.

We set up different goals to satiate our senses but derive only temporary pleasure on accomplishing them. Neuroscience has proved that pleasure is experienced in the brain when the dopamine hormone gets released in anticipation of the sensory experience. Pleasure is not experienced in the actual experience itself. This is because that was never meant to be our ultimate goal. We never tried to identify the final goal of life because we have always wrongly assumed worldly success as our life goal. Instead of exploring the world created by God, we get entangled in our self-created world.

However, the truth is that the mind and senses we use to achieve external success can also help us achieve the ultimate goal. This does not mean that whatever we have done so far towards the goal of life is in vain or wrong. Rather, it has become a ladder to reach the ultimate goal, as it has helped us train ourselves for the ultimate purpose of being on Earth.

Due to the lack of right understanding and awareness, we get deluded into pursuing attractive offers in the world. We were meant to experience enlightenment by putting our time to the best use to gain wisdom and practice mastery over our senses. We need to contemplate: What should be the goal of my life? Would I feel lasting bliss and contentment by achieving what I am pursuing today?"

We need to leverage our mind and senses to experience the supreme bliss and contentment of the true Self. When the senses are made instrumental for the Self, the journey of truth begins. In ancient times, sages would practice intensive penance to restrain and guide their senses inward to experience the true Self. Similarly, we need to coach each of our senses and guide them inward. Let us understand how to practice this.

The Eyes: When we visit a temple and get a glimpse of the sacred idol of God or get to behold the beautiful vistas of natural landscapes, our mind turns within and connects with the Source (the true Self); hence we experience joy and peace. But this peace lasts for a very short time. Our eyes start searching for the next beautiful thing. Thus, our eyes develop a tendency to pursue pleasure in the external world.

Set little reminders and stick some inspirational quotes at your home or workplace to guide your eyes inward and remind you of the real purpose. You can also place two to three little mirrors at your home or workplace. Whenever your attention wanders, look in the mirror, and ask yourself, "Who am I?" Or tell yourself, "Turn around, where is your attention right now? Is it stuck in the senses?" Or ask yourself questions that will remind you of your true Self and help you instantly dwell in the experience of your beingness.

The Nose: Observe your breathing with awareness. Be in the present without getting stuck in any fragrance or stench. Being in the present is the only way to connect with God.

As you breathe, tell yourself, "I am taking in life energy with every breath. Divine grace is permeating me. My senses are helping me align with the experience of the Self."

In this way, let your life become fragrant and blossom like a flower. Let every external fragrance or stench remind you of the inner truth. Let every sense organ become instrumental in connecting you with divinity.

The Ears: Calm down your mind to listen to the inner voice within you. For this, try to listen to every subtlest sound outside. While listening to it, look within and try to recognize the inner voice of your presence. After practicing this for a few days, you will be able to hear the echo of the silent living presence within you. As much as possible, listen to the discourses of truth and devotional music. This will help you defocus from gross sounds and turn your attention inward. You can then progress on your path to the truth.

The Tongue: Saint Kabir says, "Speak such words that liberate the mind, soothe others and yourself." This means the words you speak should glorify the dignity of speech and become the divine voice. Everyone, including you, will feel calm and pure on hearing such words.

You can guide your speech inward towards the Self with the glory of divine remembrance. By repeatedly chanting a mantra, positive energy gets generated within the body. Absorb the tongue in chanting so that the mind remains stable regardless of whatever happens outside.

Whatever you taste with the tongue should become a sacred offering. Strengthen the power of self-restraint of the tongue by not getting caught up in the lure of the taste buds.

The Skin: Let the body be in a liberating pose. Join your palms in the posture of prayer or spread your hands up towards the sky and tell yourself, "I am liberated, I am happy, I am happiness." This will help spread the vibration of peace within your body and mind.

No matter what work you engage in, keep focusing on the experience of Self. A part of a mother's attention is always on her child, even when she is busy with her work. Similarly, develop such an awareness that no matter what happens, whether in pain or pleasure, your focus will always remain on the inner experience of beingness, the experience of the true Self.

14

When the Self-realized Trains the Self

Imagine a classroom having five students, a class monitor, and a teacher. The teacher has asked the class monitor to keep an eye on the class and convey the teacher's instructions to the rest of the students. But here, the teacher is asleep and lost in her dream world. She keeps murmuring in her sleep and making some gestures with her hands. The poor monitor struggles to understand the teacher's babbles and gestures and shares whatever he has interpreted or understood with the five other students.

The students create havoc by listening to the monitor. One of the students has brought comics. He starts reading the comics by placing them inside his textbook. Another student has brought perfume and is spraying it all over. One student is chewing gum, while another is listening to music with headphones on. One student has brought a hand fan and is fanning himself. All the students and the monitor are thrilled as they believe this is what their teacher has instructed them to do. However, the teacher is lost in her dreams.

When the teacher intermittently straightens up and sits erect on her chair, the class monitor becomes alert. The other students also sit upright in their seats. There is absolute silence in the class for some time. But as soon as the teacher again dozes off, the students resume their pranks.

The teacher is half asleep at times when she sleepwalks around the class. Every student she passes by asks her to do something for him. For example, the first student says, "Clean the dirt from my ears." The second student says, "Clean the dirt from my nails." The third one says, "Something is pricking my eyes. Blow it away." The fourth student says, "Wipe my running nose." The fifth student says, "Apply some medicine to my mouth ulcers." Being half-asleep, the teacher obliges.

One day, a new principal takes charge of the school. He whispers something in the teacher's ear. Suddenly, she wakes up and instructs the monitor with her gestures. The monitor gives new instructions to the students, and the entire scene changes. The one who listens to music starts listening to the teacher. The one who is reading comics starts studying. The one who is fanning himself starts doing his homework, and the one who is chewing gum starts revising his lessons. Now, the atmosphere of the class is completely changed.

In this analogy, the five students symbolize our senses; the class monitor symbolizes the mind; the teacher is the Self (who we truly are). The principal represents the guru, the spiritual master.

Earth is also a school. We are here to learn our lessons while living in the classroom of our life. The consciousness within us, the teacher, is in a state of slumber. It is absorbed in its own experience. We have been bestowed the five senses, the mind, and the intellect, along with the body. We have to make use of these blessings to make our life blissful. Furthermore, we have to fulfill Mission Earth - our purpose of being on Earth. As the Self remains in a stupor and lacks awareness, the five senses obey the instructions of the mind and remain entangled in Maya, the illusory world.

In ignorance, the mind does whatever it wishes and makes the senses follow its diktats. They both enjoy doing so in the dark of non-awareness; hence they do not like to be aware.

Ignorant of the qualities of the Self, we blindly spend our entire life enlisting the Self to solve the mundane problems of the mind and the senses. This is like asking the genie who appears from Aladdin's magic lamp to get a little matchstick for us when it can give us anything we want. Instead of expressing the divine qualities of the Self, we get the Self to keep fulfilling our trivial desires in ignorance. If the Self is trained to overcome its stupor and remain self-aware, we can attain greater heights in life.

Later in the analogy, the principal whispered something in the teacher's ear, and everything changed. Similarly, when the self-realized guru appears in our life, he first guides us with the art of training the mind to awaken the Self. When the mind achieves the right understanding, it becomes receptive to the inner wise voice of the Self. It then becomes easy to guide our senses in the right direction. In the guru's presence, the Self is always alert and aware and treads the path of Mission Earth with the right guidance and knowledge. We can then easily safeguard ourselves from the tricky quicksand of Maya.

Life changes when the guru enters our life. Initially, we cannot perceive this change. But gradually, the more we work on the guru's teachings, we start seeing things with great clarity, and our faith in the guru deepens.

These days when there are so many gurus available, it becomes difficult to recognize the right guru for us. The Self alone helps us to identify our true guru. While going through certain incidents in life, we are often guided with some clues towards the right guru. If we are alert and there is an intense thirst of the Self to attain the right understanding, then the right guru indeed enters our life.

Just as a school peon rings the bell at school, time itself gives us the hint of the coming of the guru. The principal (guru) can enter our life in different ways and impart guidance to awaken the teacher (the Self) within us. With the awakening of the Self, our way of living and outlook toward life changes completely. The guru is the one within whom the Self has awakened and is experiencing itself; he is the one who has conquered his mind and senses. He alone can awaken the slumbering Self within us. Let us understand this with an analogy.

Once a teacher distributed sunflower seeds among his students. He asked them to sow the seeds and take care of the saplings. All the students started working on it. But one of them did not like this task.

When the sapling started growing, he lost his patience. He asked the teacher, "Can I uproot this sapling?" The teacher replied, "Let it grow; take care of it. You can get many seeds from just one sapling." However, the student did not listen to the teacher. As soon as the first seed germinated, he uprooted the sapling.

The rest of the students grew their saplings under the teacher's guidance. The student was disappointed to see the wonderful sunflower plants grown by the other children. He apologized to the teacher, "I have wasted my time and effort by ignoring your instruction. From now on, I will always be patient and follow whatever you tell me."

Knowing is one thing and putting the knowledge into practice is another. For the one who learns the art of practicing, overcoming all the challenges of life becomes easy; he attains success in all his endeavors. In fact, knowledge can be gained from experiences, successes, or even failures. Hence, we must be open and receptive to knowledge in whatever way it may come to us. We should have the highest respect for the guru who imparts the supreme and purest wisdom in our life. We can attain ultimate success in our life only when we recognize his glory through his wisdom.

If we have spent our life in Maya, and the people around us are devoid of any knowledge about the Self or its expression and are caught up in Maya, how can they guide us? They will talk of nothing other than Maya. But, if the guru has entered our life, he will impart the right wisdom for leading a life of truth while living in Maya. He will guide us to raise our level of consciousness.

We will learn how to receive this knowledge and awaken the Self in the following chapters.

15

Whom Should the Senses Listen

Everyone wants company in life. Nobody likes being alone. Imagine that God is coming to stay with you for a few days. How will your life be in God's company, every moment under God's watchful eye?

You are drinking your morning tea, and God is sitting next to you. With the first sip of tea, just as you are about to shout at your mother, "Mom, you haven't put sugar in the tea," you see God sitting in front of you. You immediately become aware and think, "God wouldn't like me yelling at my mother." So, you choose to remain calm. After drinking tea, you take a shower. And for the first time, you heartily worship God.

Then you enter your car to go to your office and see that God is seated in the passenger seat beside you. Your phone rings during your journey. You are about to answer the call while driving. But you remember that God is watching you. You park your car by the roadside and take the call. You are about to ask for a special favor from someone to do his work, but you think, "It is immoral to say this before God." Instead, you politely say, "Please come over. Your work will be done." Even in your office, you neither argue with your colleagues nor shout at your staff throughout the day. On that day, all your negative words are replaced by, "No problem! It's okay!"

This could probably be one of those rare days in your life when you abstain from backbiting, abusing, dishonesty, and deceit for the entire day.

Calling it a day, when you drive back home, you request God, "O Lord, please fasten your seat belt. You also need to follow some rules." A smile of contentment spreads on God's face. As you calmly finish your dinner, your mother chirps in amazement, "Hey, what's happened to you? Did the sun rise in the west today? You haven't pointed out a single flaw in the meal today!"

You cheerfully tell her, "Yes, Mom! The sun has risen within me today. I have been munching food mechanically all these days. But, today I had food as a sacred blessing from God, and His blessing can never be flawed."

After a stroll, you go to bed. As you rest your head on the pillow with a calm and relaxed mind, God lovingly caresses you and says, "You don't need any music, medicine, or the breeze of a fan to sleep today. You are complete all by yourself."

Now you start spending your day with God. When a thought of doing or saying something wrong arises, your inner voice immediately alerts you, "Be mindful! God is watching you." You become aware immediately. Your behavior changes day by day. You start interacting with everyone with love. You start listening to your colleague's problems, empathizing, understanding, and advising them. You treat your mother more affectionately. You spend time with her and help her with her daily chores.

Gradually, you become calm within, with no stress, no hue and cry, no screaming and shouting. Your mother is surprised to see the change in you and so are you too. You wonder, "There is so much peace and joy in life! It has never been this way before! Life is so beautiful today! No stress, no rifts! Bliss alone prevails!"

And then suddenly, you hear your mother calling out, "How long will you sleep? Wake up." And you wake up from your dream! But this dream has awakened you from a long slumber of many years. Now you understand God's indication, "You are being observed!"

A single thought, "God is watching me every moment," can stop all the senses from wandering helter-skelter. And as they stop wandering, they will be guided in the right direction. Only then will divine qualities manifest through you. You will abide by your true nature, and all actions will intuitively happen through you. All decisions taken by you will lead you in the right direction. You will be in perfect alignment with the will of God.

Everyone knows, "God is in every particle; nothing comes into action without Him." If you want to be free from the trap of your senses, try to listen to your inner voice. Our consciousness alerts us about any potential danger through our inner voice.

Today, we have become so busy with our daily chores that we rarely pause and reflect on which direction we are leading our life. Our senses lead us astray, from one desire to another, into a web of infinite desires. We chase them like an unbridled horse or a car without a steering control or brakes. While running around amid this, our consciousness often shouts from within, "Hold on! Apply the brakes. This speed is dangerous." But we are engrossed in our own tunes.

We find it a waste of time to listen to our inner voice and slow down our activities. We move ahead in our own tunes because we are in a hurry to reach somewhere. But where? We don't know! Our consciousness keeps reminding us and shouting from within for a long time. When we ignore it, it gets suppressed. But sadly, we don't realize it. Now, it is time to become free from the trap of the senses and listen to our inner voice. The inner voice always guides us on the right path, and its guidance is simple and easy.

You would have seen this often. When someone is faced with a difficult situation and cannot find a solution, he feels that all the doors are closed. At that moment, an earnest prayer arises within him, "Dear God, please guide me."

This prayer reaches God, and guidance starts flowing towards him. A strong thought may arise within him which seems perfectly justified to him. He will then begin working on it with complete faith, which will bring astonishing results. When asked, he would honestly admit that he didn't know how that thought occurred; it just came out of nowhere!

Such thoughts are called intuition, divine guidance, or inner voice. We often say, "I heard an inner voice within me," or "I got an intuition to do this." Such thoughts arise as a result of our prayers. They can be initiated either in the form of words within us or through an external hint. We become so convinced and energized by them that we are immediately prepared to act on them. They always bring positive results.

But for this, we have to recognize our inner voice and get attuned to it. Many a time, our feelings help us sense the truth in them. The inner voice communicates either through intuition, or through other means, like someone's words, pictures, or some unseen signal from nature.

Nature answers all our questions, and our feelings grasp them too. We only need to be a little aware and receptive to them. When we begin to grasp these signals and work on them, we gradually get trained in this endeavor. We start recognizing our inner voice and become receptive to the signals of nature. We get aligned with nature, with our true Self. This is the key to a simple and easy life, where we live in harmony with nature.

16

Tell Your Senses "No New News"

Imagine that you are sitting on a bench in a garden with your best friend - Anubhav. He always accompanies you wherever you go and helps you in all your endeavors. He guides you in the right direction from time to time.

In the first scene, you are sitting peacefully with Anubhav. Suddenly, you catch sight of a poster stuck on the wall in front of you. You go closer to see it. As you observe it, your attention is drawn to another beautiful poster. As you read that poster, you move on to read yet another poster, and this goes on. You keep reading one poster after another and completely forget that Anubhav is always with you.

In the second scene, you see some people scurrying across in a state of panic. You ponder and try to judge their situation and begin to follow them. Suddenly, you get a jolt when you turn back and find a gangster hot on your heels. You quickly hide behind your friend Anubhav to avoid this gangster. Once the gangster goes away, you sit on the bench with awareness and intermittently resume chatting with Anubhav.

In the third scene, you see some children playing in the garden. Soon, they start fighting with each other. But you simply look at them and peacefully sit with your friend, with an attitude of detachment.

In this analogy, you are your body, mind, intellect, and senses. Anubhav is your true Self, the sense of living presence that is always within you. Posters, people running about, and children are the various enticing attractions of Maya that swirl before your eyes day and night. Whenever you are in Maya, your mind and senses get entangled in it, and you drift away from the experience of Self.

Imagine yourself in these three scenes. Each scene depicts what your state will be. You go closer to a poster in the first scene and get engrossed in it. Then you keep moving forward, engaging in posters one after the other. This is how we get caught up in desires. We blindly crave to satiate our desires day and night without discretion. The moment one desire is satisfied, the mind craves for another, then the next, and the next, and so on. The web of desires keeps growing and engulfing us, and we remain immersed in Maya, forgetting the experience of our true Self.

In the first scene, rather, in the first state, you are entirely lost in the illusory world and have forgotten your true Self. In the quest to gratify sensory cravings, you open your mind to various avenues of input. Besides numerous negative feelings, many desires, lust, and longings also intrude into your mind and make you restless.

To get rid of this restlessness, you need to reflect on the incidents that keep you busy in this blind race without giving you time to take a pause. Only after you pause for a while can you distance yourself and get out of this blind race to achieve something new in life. You can bring awareness within you during this pause and transition from the first state to the second to scale new heights in life.

For this, first ensure that your mind does not get entangled in Maya. As soon as you are about to drift into the illusory world, immediately remind yourself, "I am getting entangled in Maya." This will alert you immediately, and you will slow down a little. This will allow you to focus your attention on the experience of the Self, though only for a few moments. Gradually, this period of awareness will increase, and you will begin to enjoy the second state, where you swing between entanglements in Maya and alignment with the experience of the Self.

In the second scene or state, just like the people running around here and there, the mind keeps vacillating between past and future thoughts. It enjoys wandering around aimlessly. It cannot live in the present because it has no role in the present. The Self alone prevails in the present and witnesses all that is happening calmly in a relaxed manner.

The mind does not like to be still. Hence, it tries to escape the present and gets preoccupied with something. The constant wandering of the mind creates stress in life. You do not feel at peace because you drift away from the experience of your true nature. When you recollect some negative incidents, you get overwhelmed with feelings of fear, guilt, or resentment. You then choose to indulge in Maya to escape these negative feelings. However, at times when you are aware, you ignore the demands of the senses and abide by the experience of the Self to safeguard yourself from Maya. But soon, the attractions of Maya overpower you so much that you start living in a stupor again.

Hence, whenever you get caught up in an illusory attraction, first practice calming down your mind and senses. Sit with yourself for a while and observe whether the senses are experiencing any stress, are they chasing something. Talk to your senses to calm them down.

Let us understand what to tell the senses and how. When the senses are stressed and driven to know something and the mind wants to wander, take two to four deep breaths and exhale slowly. If the eye demands to see something new, tell the eye with awareness, "**No New News!** Now, there is nothing to see. Relax!" Here, NEWS means North, East, West, and South. If the senses repeatedly demand something to eat, see, or hear, tell them, "No New News for you! You will not get anything from any direction. Just dwell in the experience of the Self, without reacting to anything."

So far, we have been trained by Maya to pursue news and demand sensations. But hereafter, when the mind asks for something, instead of agreeing to it, calmly let it pass by saying, "No New News!"

Imagine that you are waiting for the train at the railway station. You see some other passengers waiting for the train; some walking on the platform; some sipping tea and having snacks at the stalls; porters shifting luggage from one place to another. You peacefully watch all of them. Suddenly, you hear the announcement that your train is delayed by an hour. Your mind immediately starts complaining, and your tongue demands, "Let's eat something to pass the time. There is an hour to go." At that time, tell your tongue, "Hello dear, No New News! The train is late by an hour. Sit in peace. You will not get anything."

In this way, you can talk to your senses and train them. With training, they will stop demanding more than necessary and will gradually get accustomed to abiding in the experience of the Self. Thus, you can move towards liberation from the illusion of Maya, the mind, and the senses, and dwell in untouched bliss in the present.

In the third scene or state, all your senses fully obey you. The Self experiences itself using your body, mind, intellect, and senses as a medium. You dwell in the experience of Self regardless of whatever happens outside and witness all the external incidents, as they are, with detachment. You should resolve to attain this ultimate state and train your senses accordingly.

To attain this state, you need to consistently work on your mind and senses, practice living in the present, and be in harmony with nature. When you are aligned with nature, blessings await you every moment. Whatever you receive in the present moment is nectar. Receive it and be in the experience of the Self.

If you are sitting in a garden, the rocky ground on which you are seated is a blessing. The greenery around, the rustling sound of the wind, its cool touch, and the chirping of birds are like nectar to you. When you and your senses peacefully dwell in the experience of the

Self, the bliss, peace, and serenity you experience are like heaven! This is nature's surprise gift for you.

We warn children, "Stop your pranks, else you won't get anything. Sit quietly!" Likewise, nature is full of wonders. If you can sit in peace, wonders will unfold before you!

17

How to Master Your Senses

Once, someone asked Swami Vivekananda, "Do you feel you can attain God-realization by leading such an ascetic way of life with these people?"

Swami Vivekananda replied, "Even if I don't attain God-realization by choosing this way of life, I am fully happy and content living this way. It is indeed a truly successful life, rather than a life squandered away in the futile and incessant hankering after the illusory sensory pleasures."

This shows that it was far more important for Swami Vivekananda to attain the ultimate goal of life than to waste life being deluded in the world of senses.

Take a pause and reflect on whether you also prefer such thinking.

An ordinary person remains trapped in the vicious cycle of his mind and senses throughout his life. He believes that he can be successful only when he can fulfill all his desires easily. Though he lacks awareness, he has enough wealth, all kinds of comforts, status, and an unrestrained passion for fulfilling his desires.

He does not pause and reflect, "Why do I always crave after desires? What if I had not done what I have done so far?" He is not trained to think on these lines, and no one makes him aware of this possibility.

As a result, he leads an ordinary life being subservient to his senses and does not regret it. His mind remains entangled in the same sensory cravings even during the last moments of his life.

When we do not have complete knowledge about something, we remain deprived of its benefits. But now that we are gaining this knowledge, we have to decide how we can use our mind and senses for our highest expression so that our human birth becomes truly worthwhile. So far, we have lived a life in illusion. Now, let us guide it on the other route and learn to live accordingly.

Route means path, direction, and routine. Whenever we take a new route, we may face some difficulties; we may have to make significant changes in our life. Our mind may strongly resist this change in the beginning. It tries to pull us back into the illusory world by making various excuses. But, when someone repeatedly informs and reminds us about the new route, we initially examine that route. And once we are convinced that it is the right path, we are prepared to walk that path.

Suppose you drive to your workplace every day by a particular route. The road is wide, but it is a long way to reach the workplace. Everyone follows it, so you never think of a new route and continue to drive along the same long route.

One day your friend says, "There's another route. You must try it. It's a bit narrow for a short stretch but pretty smooth and broad after that. This new route will save you half the time you take to reach the office."

Your mind initially protests a couple of times, "No need to try new ways. The present route is fine." But one day, regardless of the mind, you travel by the new route and indeed reach your office in half the time. You also come across some new and helpful insights while driving along this route. You gain the insight that the more you drive along this new route, the easier it becomes to traverse it!

Likewise, we follow the same routine every day, so our mind and senses have become our master. They have got trained to wander in the outside world, chasing one desire after another. If we are presented with the option of a new way or a routine, the mind and senses are not prepared to adopt it immediately. We need to gain the right understanding and train ourselves to ask the right questions for this. Then we can guide our senses within. By directing them inward, we can transcend our senses to experience and express the divine qualities of the Self, like love, bliss, and peace.

A homemaker used to spend a lot of time keeping her house clean. Despite this, she remained dissatisfied and confused. She found it difficult to follow her hobbies like reading books, painting, gardening, etc. Hence, she would always feel stressed and frustrated. One day, anxious and worried, she opened her heart to her friend, "After all, why does this happen with me alone? Do I have to keep doing the same work every day? Am I going to be awarded any medal for keeping the house so clean? When will I live for myself?"

Her friend countered, "Is this house meant to serve you, or are you meant to serve the house?" She replied, "The house is meant to serve me as a shelter." Then her friend told her, "That's it! Then why are you so upset about doing these daily chores? Whatever you do, no matter how much you do, do it happily."

A new understanding dawned within her. She realized, "The house is for me to live in; I am not for this house. Then why am I stressed about managing it! I have to do all these chores for my happiness, regardless of any medal I get."

Similarly, our body is the house of the Self. We have been bestowed with the mind and senses in this body to help the Self express love, bliss, and peace in this house. However, our mind and senses find thoughts, tastes, fragrances, sounds, and scenes most pleasant and keep indulging in them. We also mistake catering to them to be our real goal. So, we get entangled in them to gratify their insatiable desires and keep suffering all our life.

Now, you need to look at your life in the light of this new understanding. Whenever the mind gets entangled, change your route, and ask yourself, "Are my senses meant to serve me, or am I meant to serve the senses?" Immediately, a new awareness will awaken within you, and your senses will not get entangled in Maya. They will not get engrossed in the mobile, TV, or backbiting for long.

Whenever you get entangled in allurements, question yourself and get liberated. Here are some examples:

- Is the mobile for me, or am I for the mobile?
- Is the work for me, or am I for the work?
- Are the things available in the market for me, or am I for them?
- Is the TV for me, or am I for the TV?
- Is the music for me, or am I for the music?
- Are the scenes for me, or am I for the scenes?
- Is the taste for me, or am I for the taste?
- Is the fragrance for me, or am I for the fragrance?

By asking such questions, a new dimension will unfold in your life. Your mind and senses will get a U-turn to dwell in the Self. In this way, lovingly guide your senses within. Engage them in the higher expression of the Self like Swami Vivekananda did, and spread love, bliss, and peace all around!

18

The State of Liberation From the Senses

Some children were playing on the seashore. Suddenly a huge wave came and took away one of the children's slippers into the sea. The child ran behind it but could not grab his slippers. He shouted at the sea, "You are a thief. You have stolen my slippers." He wrote on the sand, "The sea is a thief."

A fisherman used to earn a living by catching fish from the sea to feed his family. He also wrote on the sand, "The sea is our guardian and protector."

A youth drowned in the sea and died. His mother wrote in the sand, "The sea is a murderer."

A poor man found a pearl in an oyster from the sea. He wrote, "The sea is a benevolent donor."

And then a big wave came and wiped out everything.

In this example, we see how each one perceives the sea through the lens of their own experiences and labels it accordingly. However, the sea remains indifferent to whatever they say or write. It erases everything written on the sand in a moment and gets immersed in itself. We all know that freshwater from rivers, spring water, and even polluted water from gutters and drainages flow into the sea. Yet, the sea assimilates everything without getting affected. Similarly, the Self assimilates all kinds of experiences from our senses and yet remains detached.

Our senses create the objective world by observing the illusion outside. Then the mind superimposes its thoughts, beliefs, and past impressions, giving rise to an illusory world. This is Maya. Maya lures us throughout the day. We never realize when our thoughts draw us into the illusory world. We remain entangled in Maya for hours together. Sometimes, days, months, and even years pass, and we wander in the illusory world.

A few people in this world are like the sea. No matter how much the senses pull them, they remain unaffected. The understanding has awakened within them that, just like the sea, they can dwell in their true Self and witness the play of the senses with detachment without being swayed by them. Just as everything written on the sand is erased instantly by the sea wave, we can remain pure and unsullied by erasing all the impressions the senses have made until today and accept the new sensory inputs positively without bias.

There are two states in which we become free from the senses.

1. The first state is that of deep sleep, where we are not conscious. At night, during deep sleep, everything vanishes when the world of the senses comes to a halt. But as soon as we wake up and open our eyes, the external world of senses and the inner world of thoughts resume. We soon forget that we were abiding in the experience of the Self for so many hours. Thus, we attain a detached state during deep sleep every day, albeit unconsciously.

2. The second state is meditation. We witness everything with detachment in meditation. During meditation, we are aware, conscious, and alert. When we practice watching everything as a detached witness, we gain the conviction that we can function through our body without giving any undue importance to the senses.

When we sit in meditation, we first focus within and then gradually dive into the depth of meditation. We intuitively realize the answers to questions like:

- Why have we received this body?
- Why have we got these senses and the mind?
- What visuals should our eyes watch that can remind us of the Truth?
- What sounds should our ears listen to lead us unto the Truth?
- What taste and touch should our tongue long for to remain absorbed in the Truth?
- Which thoughts can awaken devotion within us that will dissolve all our tendencies?

Having received all these insights in meditation, we come to know, "What I have assumed myself to be till now; what I have lost in the process while life goes on like this; how I remained trapped in my own game."

In meditation, we have to invest our time, energy, and attention to go beyond our mind and senses. This is the ultimate purpose of our life. We need to make the body instrumental in witnessing the play of the mind and the senses with detachment without getting stuck in them.

For example, while watching a show on TV, if your attention gets diverted to the chorus actors dancing in the background, turn your attention back to the main hero. This is what you have to practice during meditation. When your attention gets diverted to the myriad sensory inputs and thoughts of the mind, turn your attention back to the living presence within, which is the only hero, without which nothing can be! The mind and senses wander here and there, but you must guide them back into meditation.

The State of Liberation from the Senses

Let us practice A-B-C-D meditation and free ourselves from the captivity of the mind and senses to attain the state of liberation. Before closing your eyes, read and understand the instructions first.

1. Choose a quiet place and sit calmly with closed eyes. Now focus your attention on A.

2. **A - Inner blocks and difficulties:** Bring into your awareness the problems that agitate you and disturb your peace. Contemplate, in which areas have your senses created complications or difficulties in your life? What problems have you faced because of them? Are you able to experience the Self amidst all of this?

3. **B - Be the sea:** To "be the sea" means to be like the sea and completely detach yourself. Identify the cause of your problems and restlessness and surrender it to the Self during meditation. Just as everything dissolves in the sea, you also remain absorbed in the untouched experience of the Self and dissolve in it.

   When you go a little farther from the seashore and write something on the sand, it remains intact for a long time because the waves cannot reach there. Instead, if you write something on the beach by the seashore, it gets erased by the waves immediately. Similarly, when you dwell in the experience of the Self, your life becomes easy, simple, and pure. As soon as a problem occurs, it subsides immediately. But when you drift away from the experience of the Self, problems seem to loom large in your life. If it is not possible to be the sea, i.e., dwell in the experience of the Self, take the next step.

4. **C - See clearly:** See (watch) the incidents, difficulties, and blocks clearly. Close the fist of one of your hands so tight as if you have caught the difficulty. Now ask yourself, "I want to witness my wrong belief in this incident that is making it appear as a difficulty to me. What is the subtle desire and attachment of the senses that is posing a hurdle in tiding through this situation?" Observe clearly.

5. **D - Declare, Delete, Dissolve:** Ask yourself, "Can I open my fist and let go of this problem that I am holding onto? Can I dissolve it?" If the answer is "Yes," open your fist and tell yourself, "Declared, Dissolved, Deleted."

6. In this way, dissolve the problems causing you stress due to entanglement in the senses in the sea of meditation. When you experience a feeling of completeness, open your eyes.

Be aware that your senses don't drag you into Maya. Many allurements may come, desires may arise, and cravings may pull you in, but repeatedly abide by the Self during meditation. This will guide your senses in the right direction. And yet, if the senses draw your attention, they won't be that intense to delude you. Everything falls into place when you have complete faith in the power of meditation and prayer.

Appendix
The Complete Meditation of the Senses

God has blessed all living beings with the gift of senses at their birth. The primary duty of the senses is to fulfill body's physical needs and protect it. This happens intuitively in all living beings. But humans have been blessed with something more along with the senses due to which they can think, enjoy, invent, and admire the Creator's creation.

The human mind starts watching the world in amazement from childhood and gradually races outward. The senses begin to perceive color, form, taste, fragrance, touch, sound, etc. Consequently, they begin to crave these sensory experiences and keep aspiring for more.

For example, the eyes watch something, but they are always curious to see what's next. The tongue tastes something, but it wants to know the taste of the next thing it will eat. Thus, each sense anticipates the next sensory input and wants to enjoy it but cannot do so because it has to live with the body. That's why the senses are always under stress. For example, if the ear doesn't hear any music, it yearns for it and remains tense until it hears something that it is looking out for.

Each sense is always under some form of stress. If they are told to do nothing and assured that doing nothing will bring about a transformation in them, they will be stressed about that too. They will keep checking whether this transformation is really happening or keep wondering when it will happen.

Now, we have to learn the art of reducing the stress on the senses and bringing them into a relaxed state. It is similar to the way the *gopis* (the milkmaids of Gokul) would be relieved of stress and remain absorbed in the divine tune of Lord Krishna's flute. They would not bother about having food, enjoying anything, or going anyplace. They would be so absorbed in the tune of the flute that they would dwell in the state of absolute stillness, being oblivious to everything else.

We can also achieve this state when the senses stop hankering after sensory pleasures in the external world and remain at rest. They need to find something better within us than the material world outside for that.

One may question, "We relax our senses every night during deep sleep. Even when we practice yoga every day, we relax them during yogic sleep (*Yoga Nidra*). Then what more relaxation do they need?" But contemplate deeply, "Do you feel refreshed on waking up every morning?" Most people will say, "No," because whatever inputs are assimilated through the senses during the day manifest as dreams in sleep. Yoga Nidra and relaxation give temporary rest to the senses. But here, we are talking about permanent relaxation by training the senses through meditation.

Let us now practice a meditation to relax our senses. Your life will become easy, simple, beautiful, and blissful as you practice this meditation regularly. By relaxing the senses, their quality will improve, and they will truly become a blessing. This meditation holds the key to a stress-free life. Read and understand it first before practicing.

Appendix

1. Choose a comfortable posture and sit in meditation with your eyes closed.

2. Keep your body still and listen to the sounds around you. Identify at least five different sounds. Do not rush to identify them. Instead of trying to reach out to the sounds, let the sounds reach you. With a calm mind, shift your attention from one sound to another. Listen and try to identify them without getting stuck to any one sound. Whether the sound is gross or subtle, loud or soft, listen to it and move on. When there is no sound, try to know the sound of silence and experience tranquility.

3. After listening to the sounds, focus your attention on the environment. Feel the touch of the air around you. Feel the heat, cold, dryness, or humidity in the air. Feel the lightness or heaviness on the body. Notice all the sensations your skin can sense.

4. Now focus your attention on the body. Experience and feel any stiffness or pain in the body. While perceiving the pain in the body, remain still without any movement. Experience sensations in the entire body - be it heaviness or lightness, the touch of clothes or air on the body, itching, burning, dryness, sweating, etc. Thus, witness all severe and subtle sensations on and within the body.

5. In meditation, "to watch" or "to witness" implies "to know." Don't imagine anything while knowing. Just feel the sensations within and on the body. Don't escape from whatever is happening in the present; just attend to them. Witness the experiences as they are, without labeling them as good or bad.

6. Now focus your attention on your breathing. Witness how the breathing is going on naturally. From which nostril air

is being inhaled, and from which nostril it is exhaled. Just watch every breath you inhale and exhale, whether warm or cool, shallow or deep, calm or rapid.

7. Now slowly open your eyes. Take a moment to look at any colorful object in the room. Again, close your eyes and attentively observe whether you see only that colorful object or something else. If you see the same object, it is the power of focus! When you focus your attention and eyes only on one object, it gets imprinted in your brain as a picture.

8. Now shift your attention to the tongue. Observe whether the tongue holds any taste or retains any words about anything or anyone. During meditation, the tongue is usually calm and free of any taste. It neither instigates you to say anything nor asks for anything to eat. You can continue experimenting this with awareness even after meditation. During the day, whenever your tongue craves to eat some unnecessary food or abuse someone, immediately remind it that it can remain calm even without resorting to these things.

9. Now shift your focus from the tongue to the thoughts going on in your mind and know them. After knowing one thought, let it pass by silently saying "Next" and move on to the next thought that arises. If a thought arises, "There is no thought," then know that this too is a thought. On witnessing it, let it pass by and silently say, "Next." As you remain still and keep witnessing the thoughts, you will experience the joy of detachment from your thoughts.

10. In this way, witness all your senses with awareness during this meditation. Stay in this state for a while. Then slowly open your eyes. Continue to dwell in the same experience as you walk around with open eyes. Observe all the senses when the body is amid activity.

As you begin to recognize the relaxed state of awareness in meditation, your mind becomes calm, and so do the senses. Now the mind will not be affected by anything. Next time, when a thought arises in your mind, witness it and smile.

Just as it is necessary to take a bath daily, so it is with the practice of meditation. Practice this meditation daily, and the slate of your mind will be cleansed. Otherwise, the mind becomes tense when it is filled with the clutter of desires and cravings. This meditation will relieve you of stress and establish you in the bliss of Self-realization.

❖ ❖ ❖

You can mail your opinion or feedback on this book to: books.feedback@tejgyan.org

Write for Us

We welcome writers, translators and editors to join our team. If you would like to volunteer, please email us at: englishbooks@tejgyan.org or call : +91 90110 10963

About Sirshree

Sirshree's spiritual quest, which began during his childhood, led him on a journey through various schools of thought and prevalent meditation practices. His overpowering desire to attain the Truth made him relinquish his teaching profession. After a long period of contemplation on the truth of life, his spiritual quest culminated in the attainment of the ultimate truth. Since then, over the last two decades, he has dedicated his life toward elevating mass consciousness and making spiritual pursuit simple and accessible to all.

Sirshree espouses, **"All paths that lead to the truth begin differently, but culminate at the same point – understanding. Understanding is complete in itself. Listening to this understanding is enough to attain the truth."**

Sirshree has delivered more than 3000 discourses that throw light on this understanding, simplify various aspects of life and unravel missing links in spirituality. He delivers the understanding in casual contemporary language by weaving profound aspects into analogies, parables and humor that provoke one to contemplate.

To make it possible for people from all walks of life to directly experience this understanding, Sirshree has designed the *Maha Aasmani Param Gyan Shivir* – a retreat designed as a comprehensive system for imparting wisdom. This system for wisdom, which has been accredited with ISO 9001:2015 certification, has inspired thousands of seekers from all walks of life to progress on their journey of the Truth. This system makes the wisdom accessible to every human being, regardless of religion, caste, social strata, country or belief system.

Sirshree is the founder of Tej Gyan Foundation, a no-profit organization committed to raising mass consciousness with branches in India, the United States, Europe and Asia-Pacific. Sirshree's retreats have transformed the lives of thousands and his teachings have inspired various social initiatives for raising global consciousness.

His published work includes more than 150 books, some of which have been translated in more than 10 languages and published by leading publishers. Sirshree's books provide profound and practical reading on existential subjects like emotional maturity, harmony in relationships, developing self-belief, overcoming stress and anxiety, and dealing with the question of life-beyond-death, to name a few. His literature on core spirituality expounds the deeper meaning of self-realization and self-stabilization, unravelling missing links in the understanding of karma, wisdom, devotion, meditation and consciousness.

Various luminaries and celebrities like His Holiness the Dalai Lama, publishers Mr. Reid Tracy, Ms. Tami Simon and Yoga Master Dr. B. K. S. Iyengar have released Sirshree's books and lauded his work. "The Source" book series, authored by Sirshree, has sold over 10 million copies in 5 years. His book, "The Warrior's Mirror", published by Penguin, was featured in the Limca Book of Records for being released on the same day in 11 languages.

Tejgyan... The Road Ahead
What is Tejgyan?

Tejgyan is the wisdom of the existential truth, which is beyond duality. "Gyan" is a term commonly used for "knowledge". Tejgyan is the wisdom beyond knowledge and ignorance. It is understanding that arises from direct experience of the final truth. It is what sets us free from the limitations of the mind and opens us to our highest potential.

In today's world, there are people who feel disharmony and are desperately trying to achieve balance in an unpredictable life. Tejgyan helps them in harmonizing with their true nature, the Self, thereby restoring balance in all aspects of their lives.

And then, there are those who are successful, but feel a sense of emptiness within. Tejgyan provides them fulfilment and helps them to embark on a journey towards self-realization. There are others who feel lost and are seeking the meaning of life. Tejgyan helps them to realize the true purpose of human life.

All this is possible with Tejgyan due to a very simple reason. The experience of the ultimate truth (God or Pure consciousness) is always available. The direct experience of this truth is possible provided the right method is known. Tejgyan is that method, that understanding.

The understanding of Tejgyan makes it possible to lead a life of freedom from fear, worry, anger and stress. It helps in attaining physical vitality, emotional strength and stability, harmony in relationships, financial freedom and spiritual progress.

At Tej Gyan Foundation, Sirshree imparts this understanding through a System for Wisdom – a series of retreats that guides participants step by step towards realizing the true Self, being established in the experience of self-realization, and expressing its qualities. This system for wisdom has been accredited with the ISO 9001:2015 certification.

Maha Aasmani Param Gyan Shivir

"**Maha Aasmani Param Gyan Shivir**" is the flagship Self-realization retreat offered by Tej Gyan Foundation. The teachings of the retreat are non-denominational (secular).

This residential retreat is held for 3 to 5 days at the foundation's MaNaN Ashram amidst the glory of the mountains and the pristine beauty of nature. The Ashram is located at the outskirts of the city of Pune in India, and is well connected by air, road and rail. The retreat is also held at other centres of Tej Gyan Foundation across the world.

You can participate in this retreat to attain ageless wisdom through a unique System for Wisdom so that you can:

1. Discover "Who am I" through direct experience.
2. Learn to abide in pure consciousness while functioning in the world, allowing the qualities of consciousness like peace, love, joy, compassion, abundance and creativity to manifest.
3. Acquire simple tools to use in everyday life, which help quiet the chattering mind.
4. Get practical techniques to be in the present and connect to the source of all answers within (the inner guru).
5. Discover missing links in the practices of Meditation (*Dhyana*), Action (*Karma*), Wisdom (*Gyana*) and Devotion (*Bhakti*).
6. Understand the nature of your body-mind mechanism to attain freedom form its tendencies.
7. Learn practical methods to shift from mind-centered living to consciousness-centered living.

A Mini-retreat is also conducted, especially for teenagers (14 to 16 years of age) during summer and winter vacations.

To register for retreats, visit www.tejgyan.org,
contact (+91) 9921008060, or email mail@tejgyan.com

About Tej Gyan Foundation

Tej Gyan Foundation (TGF) was established with the mission of creating a highly evolved society through all-round development of every individual that transforms all the facets of their lives. It is a non-profit organization, founded on the teachings of Sirshree.

The Foundation has received the ISO certification (ISO 9001:2015) for its system of imparting wisdom. It has centres all across India as well as in other countries. The motto of Tej Gyan Foundation is 'Happy Thoughts'.

At the core of the philosophy of Tejgyan is the Power of Acceptance. Acceptance has profound meaning and is at the core of our Being. It is Acceptance that brings forth true love, joy and peace.

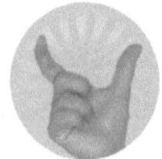

Symbol of Acceptance

The Symbol of Acceptance – shown above – is a representation of this truth. The symbol represents brackets. Whatever occurs in life falls within these brackets that signify acceptance of whatever is. Hence, this symbol forms the centerpiece of the Foundation's MaNaN Ashram.

The Foundation is creating a highly evolved society through:
- Tejgyan Programs (Retreats, YouTube Webcasts)
- Tejgyan Books and Apps
- Tejgyan Projects (Value education, Women empowerment, Peace initiatives)

The Foundation undertakes projects to elevate the level of consciousness among students, youth, women, senior citizens, teachers, doctors, leaders, professionals, corporate and Government organizations, police force, prisoners etc.

Good News!

Maha Aasmani Param Gyan Retreat
is now conducted ONLINE!

You can participate in the retreat from the convenience of your home. The retreat is conducted in 3 parts during weekends:

1. The Foundation Truth retreat

2. The Bright Responsibility retreat

3. The Maha Aasmani final retreat

For more details, please call: +91 9921008060, +91 9921008075

To register, visit: https://www.tejgyanglobal.org/mareg

Books can be delivered at your doorstep by registered post or courier. You can request the same through postal money order or pay by VPP. Please send the money order to either of the following two addresses:

WOW Publishings Pvt. Ltd.

1. Registered Office: S. No. 1A, Irani Market, Building No. D-38, Yerawada, Pune – 411006.

Phone No: (+91) 9011013210

You can also order your copy at the online store:

www.gethappythoughts.org

*Free Shipping plus 10% Discount on purchases above Rs. 500/-

For further details contact:

Tejgyan Global Foundation
Registered Office:
Happy Thoughts Building, Vikrant Complex, Near Tapovan Mandir, Pimpri, Pune 411017, Maharashtra, India.
Contact No: 020-27411240, 27412576
Email: mail@tejgyan.com

MaNaN Ashram:
Survey No. 43, Sanas Nagar, Nandoshi gaon, Kirkatwadi Phata, Sinhagad Road, Tal. Haveli, Dist. Pune 411024, Maharashtra, India.
Contact No: 992100 8060.

Hyderabad: 9885558100, Bangalore: 9880412588,
Delhi : 9891059875, Nashik: 9326967980, Mumbai: 9373440985

For accessing our unique 'System for Wisdom' from self-help to self-realization, please follow us on:

	Website Online Shopping/ Blog	www.tejgyan.org www.gethappythoughts.org
	Video Channel	www.youtube.com/tejgyan For Q&A videos: http://goo.gl/YA81DQ
	Social networking	www.facebook.com/tejgyan
	Social networking	www.twitter.com/sirshree
	Internet Radio	http://www.tejgyan.org/internetradio.aspx

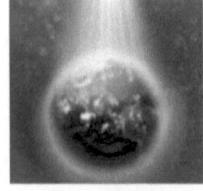

Pray for World Peace along with thousands of others every day at 09:09am and 09:09pm

Divine Light of Love, Bliss and Peace is Showering;
The Golden Light of Higher Consciousness is Rising;
All negativity on Earth is Dissolving;
Everyone is in Peace and Blissfully Shining;
O God, Gratitude for Everything!

www.ingramcontent.com/pod-product-compliance
Lightning Source LLC
LaVergne TN
LVHW041854070526
838199LV00045BB/1602